simply**healthy**

The Victor Chang Cardiac Research Institute Cookbook

Managing Editor: Rachel Blackmore
Editorial Assistance: Margaret Kelly
Consultant Dietitian: Clare Rawcliffe
Recipe Analysis: Terri Sullivan

DESIGN AND PRODUCTION
Production Director: Anna Maguire
Design Manager: Drew Buckmaster
Production Coordinator: Meredith Johnston
Production Artist: Petra Rode
Junior Production Editor: Heather Straton

PHOTOGRAPHY AND STYLING
Photographer: William Meppem
Food Stylist: Kristen Anderson
Food Stylist's Assistants: Helen Anderson, Michaela Le Compte
Styling credits: The publisher and author would like to thank the
following companies who kindly supplied the plates, glasses and
accessories shown in the photographs in this book: David Jones;
Dinosaur Designs; Eighteen Ten; Empire Homewares; Inne/Transform;
Jedo's Beach House; Made in Japan; Orson & Blake; Papaya Studio;
Plane Tree Farm; The Bay Tree; Wheel & Barrow.

Published by J.B. Fairfax Press, an imprint of LibertyOne Limited
Level 2, 80 McLachlan Avenue
Rushcutters Bay NSW 2011 Australia
A.C.N. 081 709 882
www.jbfp.com.au

Formatted by J.B. Fairfax Press
Printed by Toppan Printing Co, Hong Kong, Ltd.
PRINTED IN HONG KONG

JBFP 519
Includes Index
ISBN 1 86343 347 3

DISTRIBUTION AND SALES
J.B. Fairfax Press
Ph: (02) 9361 6366 Fax: (02) 9360 6262
Email: info@jbfp.com.au

AUTHOR'S ACKNOWLEDGMENTS

A cookbook is never just the work of one person. In fact, I believe the
'behind the scenes' workers are every bit as vital in the making of a
cookbook as the author. Each of the following people played an
important role in this cookbook, no matter how small, and I couldn't
have done it without them. My sincerest thanks to them all.

To the publishers, J.B. Fairfax Press who gave me this wonderful
opportunity. In particular, Stephen Balme who shared my vision that it
could work and Rachel Blackmore, my tireless and intuitive editor, for
her encouragement, advice and patience with my pushing deadlines to
their limit.

To Jan Savage, Ann Chang, Professor Robert Graham and the board of
the Victor Chang Cardiac Research Institute for believing in the need
for this book and offering their support. And to the memory of Victor
Chang – may his inspirations continue always.

To my loyal and hard working band of happy kitchen helpers and
tasters – my sister and her family – Wendy, Jaime, Andrew and
Stephanie who also helped make it fun, and Robert for lending them to
me; my ever-willing Mum and my Dad for his belief in me and
unwavering support and pride that is so treasured. And to Jodie and
Noel Parrish, Bernie and Fay Tucker and the band of Wentworth Falls
bus drivers who endured many 'tastings' and gave honest feedback.

To an absolutely brilliant, skilled and creative food styling and
photographic team without whom this book wouldn't be half what it is.
Thank you so much Kristen Anderson and William Meppem, for turning
my recipes into magical visions.

To Clare Rawcliffe, for her practical and perceptive nutrition advice on
my recipes, all done with such a gentle and friendly manner.

To Dr Hosen Kiat, an inspired Cardiologist, for his practical scientific
advice and popping little rays of sunshine into my days when I became
'over-consumed'.

To Sam Gordon at the Master Fish Merchants Association and Paul at
Penrith Seafoods for the freshest variety of seafood for me to play and
experiment with.

And finally, to God for all our wonderful produce, for giving me the skills
to write this book, a career I love, and such a supportive and nice team
of colleagues to work with.

simply**healthy**

The Victor Chang Cardiac Research Institute Cookbook

Sally James

Photography by William Meppem
Styling by Kristen Anderson

jbfp

contents

the Victor Chang story

Victor Chang (Yam Him) was born in Shanghai in 1936 of Australian born Chinese parents. He came to Australia in 1953 to complete his schooling at Christian Brothers College, Lewisham, and then moved on to medical training at Sydney University. Graduating in 1962, he became an intern and later a registrar in cardiothoracic surgery at St Vincent's Hospital. After completing additional training in England, and then at the prestigious Mayo Clinic in the US, he returned to St Vincent's Hospital in 1972 to join the elite St Vincent's cardiothoracic team that already included Henry Winsor and Mark Shanahan.

A pioneer of the modern era of heart transplantation, Victor Chang established the National Heart Transplant Unit at St Vincent's Hospital in 1984. During the 1980s, he became widely known as a man of vision; as a caring surgeon, as a researcher and as an ambassador for Australia and the people of South-East Asia. During this time, he nurtured a vision to establish an internationally-recognised cardiac research centre at St Vincent's and in 1990, he and others launched the "Heart of St Vincent's Appeal". With his tragic and untimely death in Sydney on July 4 1991, efforts to realise Victor Chang's dream accelerated and resulted in generous donations from the Federal Government, Mr Kerry Packer, AC, and the Australian public. With these funds, St Vincent's Hospital established the Victor Chang Cardiac Research Institute, which was launched on February 15, 1994 by the Prime Minister of Australia, the Hon Paul Keating, with Mr Kerry Packer as its Patron and Professor Robert Graham as its Director. On February 27, 1995, the Institute was incorporated as an independent research facility with the Hon Neville Wran, AC, QC, as its Chairman, and on November 1, 1996, Diana, Princess of Wales opened the Institute in its new premises.

The Institute is now a partner of the St Vincent's Campus and is affiliated with the University of New South Wales. In addition to conducting fundamental heart research, it is committed to providing excellence in cardiovascular research training and in facilitating the rapid application of research discoveries to patient care.

introduction

Yes, obesity is a major problem and an important risk factor for premature heart disease. But the good news is, if you follow the wonderful, yet healthy, recipes that Sally James presents here you don't have to 'starve yourself to death to live a little longer'.

Committed to heart health, the Victor Chang Cardiac Research Institute has undertaken to develop this cookbook as a vehicle for not only addressing the problems of existing heart disease, but as a means of preventing it.

Diseases of the heart and blood vessels remain the major cause of death in developed countries and, indeed, it is likely that early in the next millennium, heart disease, for the first time ever, will become the major killer worldwide. Excessive fat intake and obesity are important contributors. Our increasingly sedentary lifestyles, and greater reliance on fast-foods, further compound the problem.

Almost every day I see heart-attack victims, who are 'born-again' after their illness, and finally change to a healthy diet and start exercising. What a pity we can't do this before losing some of our vital, irreplaceable heart muscle. We hope the Victor Chang Cardiac Research Institute cookbook serves as a reminder that we all need to modify our diets and exercise today. Each recipe has been carefully checked by Clare Rawcliffe, Dietitian, St Vincent's Hospital, and relevant nutritional information is provided. Importantly, we have specifically designed this cookbook to be not just a static collection of tasty heart-healthy recipes, but to provide you with the opportunity to receive additional information on food and healthy eating, exercise, and your heart through the Victor Chang Cardiac Research Institute web site (see box below). Comments and suggestions for improvements or changes are also welcome.

We hope you will enjoy and use this book frequently, and join us as a partner in our efforts to improve the heart health of all.

Finally, I would like to take this opportunity to thank all involved in developing this cookbook, including not only Sally James and Clare Rawcliffe, but also J.B. Fairfax Press and, in particular, its Managing Editor, Rachel Blackmore and Marketing Director, Stephen Balme.

For questions, suggestions, comments, changes and even criticisms, please access the Victor Chang Cardiac Research Institute Cookbook on our web-site at **www.victorchang.com.au**

ROBERT M. GRAHAM, MD, FRACP, FACP
Executive Director
Victor Chang Cardiac Research Institute

simply healthy eating

We all know what we eat affects our health, but many of us are confused about what 'healthy eating' really means. We are constantly bombarded with nutritional information, often conveying conflicting messages. The truth is we don't know all the answers yet, and there will continue to be much debate over some food-related health issues. However, there are many other nutrition facts that have been scientifically proven.

The Australian Dietary Guidelines have been developed based on the latest nutrition research. They are a useful guide for people to make wise choices to help prevent nutrition related diseases.

1. enjoy a wide variety of nutritious foods

Aim to eat a mixture of foods across a whole range of food types, such as fruit, vegetables, breads, cereals, meat, fish and dairy products. Also vary your choice of foods within each of these food types. For example, breads can be wheat, rye, oat, pumpernickel, focaccia, Turkish or raisin. Eating a wide variety of foods is more likely to provide you with the essential nutrients in a more balanced proportion – carbohydrate, protein and fat as well as vitamins and minerals.

Varying your food choices helps stimulate your interest in food as well as your taste buds. Eating a varied diet means you are always changing foods, trying new ones, experimenting with different ethnic foods and cooking in different ways. Ideally, 20-30 different types of food should be eaten each day.

Ways to increase food variety

- *Vary your choice of vegetables and the way in which you eat them – sometimes raw as in salads and sometimes cooked.*

- *Try different fruits – include fresh, canned and dried.*

- *Vary your choice of bread and what you do with it – try different low-fat spreads, chutneys, jams, mustards or avocado instead of butter or margarine.*

- *Vary your choice of breakfast cereal – try wheat- or oat-based cereals with added toasted seeds, nuts and dried fruits.*

- *Vary your choice of protein foods at the evening meal – fish, legumes, beef, pork, lamb or chicken.*

- *Don't forget herbs and spices – they add flavour, colour and variety as well as sometimes providing other beneficial effects. For example, ginger can be useful in the treatment of travel sickness.*

2. eat a diet low in fat, and in particular low in saturated fat

This guideline is particularly relevant to heart disease. Eating too much fat is a major cause of overweight and obesity. Eating too much saturated fat tends to raise blood cholesterol levels. High blood cholesterol is one of the major risk factors for heart disease.

There are three types of fat in food: saturated, mono-unsaturated and polyunsaturated. All fatty foods are actually a mixture of these three types. However, foods are classified according to the type of fat present in the largest amount.

SATURATED FATS
Tend to raise blood cholesterol levels. Foods high in saturated fat include fatty meats, full-cream dairy products, coconut, and the fats used for commercial deep-frying (i.e. takeaway foods, processed foods, commercial cakes, biscuits and pastries – palm oil is a saturated fat commonly used). If you have a high blood cholesterol level you should therefore try to cut down on these foods.

TRANS FATS

Are a small class of fats found in the fat of dairy products, some meats, commercial frying oils and some margarine. Trans fats tend to raise blood cholesterol levels. They have now been removed from many margarines in Australia – look for a brand with less than 1% trans fats.

POLYUNSATURATED FATS

Tend to help lower blood cholesterol levels. These fats come mostly from vegetable oils like grapeseed, safflower and corn oil, nuts, and many margarines.

A particular type of polyunsaturated fat called Omega-3 has been found to reduce coronary risk in other ways. These fats reduce the tendency of blood to clot, help lower blood triglyceride levels, and help protect the heart from arrhythmia (an irregular heart beat). Omega-3 fats are found in seeds and seed oils and in particular in fish. It is recommended that you eat fish at least two or three times a week.

MONOUNSATURATED FATS

Also help lower blood cholesterol levels. These fats come mostly from olive and canola oils and margarine as well as oils made from nuts such as peanut oil.

Refer to page 185 for more information about blood cholesterol levels.

There is considerable debate about which type of fat is best. There are many factors to consider, but studies so far indicate that monounsaturated and polyunsaturated fats are equivalent in terms of their potential to reduce coronary risk. The most important aim should be to lower your saturated and trans fats intake. Both mono-unsaturated and polyunsaturated fats are better choices.

Remember all types of fats are equally fattening. If one of your goals is to lose weight, then you need to limit the total amount of all fat including these 'good' fats.

Another area of controversy is how much fat is acceptable, particularly if you are not overweight. Some experts state that we should limit all types of fats. Others argue that if the majority of fat eaten is unsaturated, then we can eat higher amounts of fat. The debate continues, but probably most Australians need to think in terms of limiting their total fat intake so that about 25-30% of kilojoules (calories) come from fat. This would be equivalent to:

> 40-70 g fat a day for most women and children

> 50-100 g fat a day for most men

If you want to estimate how much fat you are eating, buy a small 'Fat counter' from your local bookshop. A healthy fat intake is based on your energy needs, your age and activity levels. Younger or very active people can eat more fat than those who are older or less active.

To lose weight, estimate how much fat you are eating currently and aim to eat less than this. You may need to aim for less than 40 g a day. If you are underweight, or choose to eat more fat than this, then it is best to choose unsaturated fats e.g. nuts, seeds and avocado.

Tips for trimming fat

- Steer clear of fried takeaway foods – the type of fat/oil used is often palm oil (saturated fat).

- Choose cakes and biscuits that are low in fat and contain unsaturated fat. Home baked using unsaturated fat/oil, or commercial products that are either low-fat and/or the type of fat is clearly unsaturated (not 'vegetable oil' which will commonly be palm oil).

- Choose healthy snacks such as fresh fruit, dried fruit, bread sticks and pretzels rather than potato crisps or corn chips. Nuts are healthy too, but go easy if you need to lose weight.

- Choose low-fat or reduced-fat dairy products: milk and yogurt with 1.5 g fat per 100 g or less; cheese with 10 g fat per 100 g or less; ice cream with 5 g fat per 100 g or less.

- Choose lean cuts of meats and remove the skin from poultry. Go easy on your serve size. There is no need to avoid red meat – it is an excellent source of iron.

- Eat more fish, including canned varieties.

- Go easy on the amount of margarine you use on bread and toast – one level teaspoon per slice is ample. For a change, use avocado, cottage cheese, chutney or mustard instead.

- Go easy on the amount of oil you use in cooking. Use low-fat cooking methods such as grilling, microwaving, boiling, steaming and barbecuing and use nonstick pans.

- Remember fruit, vegetables, breads and cereals are mostly very low-fat foods and when they do contain fat, it is the unsaturated type.

3. eat plenty of breads, cereals, vegetables and fruits

The aim of this guideline is to increase your consumption of carbohydrate (starchy) foods. These foods are the main source of dietary fibre and are naturally low in fat and kilojoules (calories). They are filling, but they are not fattening – potatoes are not fattening but the butter, margarine or sour cream you add is!

All your meals should be based around carbohydrate foods and consist mostly of them. For example, a meal of spaghetti bolognese should be comprised of lots of pasta with just a small amount of meat sauce for flavour and don't forget the large side salad and crusty bread as accompaniments.

Most carbohydrate foods contain fibre, but some have more than others. You should aim to eat about 30 g fibre from a variety of sources each day. Increase the fibre in your diet gradually. This will help prevent you feeling bloated as well as experiencing excess 'wind'. Remember to drink plenty of fluids – aim for 8 glasses/ 2 litres a day, unless your doctor advises a fluid restriction for medical reasons.

There are two main types of fibre – soluble and insoluble.

SOLUBLE FIBRE
Helps lower blood cholesterol and control blood sugar levels. Good sources of soluble fibre include:

oats – rolled oats, oat bran, and oat-based cereals and breads;

legumes – peas, split peas, lentils, chickpeas, soy beans and baked beans;

some fruits – in particular apples, strawberries and citrus fruits;

barley; and

psyillium – a gummy type of dietary fibre obtained from the husk or seed of psyillium.

INSOLUBLE FIBRE
Helps prevent and control bowel problems such as constipation and diverticular disease. It is probably also related to the prevention of some types of cancer, in particular cancer of the bowel. Good food sources of insoluble fibre include:

wholegrain breads and cereals – wheat-based cereals, unprocessed wheat bran, wholegrain bread, brown rice and wholemeal pasta; and

fruits and vegetables – in particular the skins and seeds where appropriate.

Another good reason to include plenty of breads, cereals, fruits and vegetables is that these foods contain antioxidants. Antioxidants are compounds which occur naturally in plant foods and have many functions including preventing food spoilage and loss of colour and flavour. Antioxidants also have a role in the prevention of heart disease, cancer and other degenerative diseases.

There are about 600 antioxidants. These include some vitamins (A, C and E), minerals (selenium and zinc), and various other compounds such as flavanoids, phenols and glutathione. Eating a variety of foods, in particular fruits and vegetables, including nuts and seeds, ensures a mix of antioxidants which gives you the most beneficial effect. Red wine and tea (all types) are also known to be good sources of antioxidants.

Taking vitamin supplements in large doses has not been proven to be beneficial, although continuing research may prove otherwise.

Aim to eat at least two to three serves of fruit, at least four to five serves of vegetables and at least five serves of bread and/or cereal each day.

Ways to increase carbohydrate and fibre intake
- Start your day with a fibre-rich cereal (e.g. rolled oats, natural muesli or whole wheat cereal).

- Include fresh fruit or a fruit compote at breakfast, or add dried fruit to your cereal.

- Snack on fresh or dried fruit during the day.

- Have a bread-based lunch – preferably wholegrain bread with lean meat, chicken or fish and lots of salad.

- For a lunch change choose: pasta with a low-fat sauce and a salad or; baked beans on toast or; soup made with lots of vegetables and some pasta, rice or legumes and served with bread or toast.

- Eat lots of vegetables or salad at your main meal and finish with a fruit-based dessert.

- Try one of the delicious legume recipes in this book.

4. maintain a healthy body weight by balancing physical activity and food intake

Ideally, you should aim to keep your weight within the healthy weight range. Being overweight is a risk factor for many diseases including heart disease. It is well known that maintaining a healthy weight helps optimise blood cholesterol levels and blood pressure.

One way of assessing whether or not you are overweight is to calculate your Body Mass Index (BMI).

$$BMI = \frac{your\ weight\ (kg)}{your\ height^2\ (m)}$$

For example – someone who is 160 cm tall and weighs 55 kg would calculate their BMI in the following way:

$$BMI = \frac{55}{1.6\ x\ 1.6} = \frac{55}{2.56} = 21.5$$

A BMI of 20-25 is considered acceptable.

Another important consideration is body fat distribution. Fat above the hips carries a far greater health risk than fat on or below the hips. It is better to be a 'pear shape' than an 'apple shape'. Excess abdominal fat greatly increases the risk of heart disease, diabetes, high blood lipids, hypertension, stroke and some cancers.

Desirable waist circumference

Males – less than 90 cm
Females – less than 80 cm

If you are overweight, it is important to remember you are aiming to lose body fat not muscle. In the first fortnight, weight loss is often rapid, due mainly to fluid loss. Thereafter, slow weight loss is best – aim to lose a maximum of 0.5-1 kg a week.

People who exercise regularly lose more weight and keep it off longer. Regular exercise helps maintain muscle mass – therefore, as you lose weight, you lose body fat not muscle. Exercise also helps increase your metabolic rate – your body burns more kilojoules (calories). Exercise does not have to be strenuous to help you get to a healthy weight or to be good for your heart. Start off slowly and gradually build up. A little is better than none. Choose something you enjoy doing – you are more likely to keep doing it! Walking, swimming and cycling are excellent activities which will not put a strain on your body. For best weight control results you will probably need to exercise daily for 30-40 minutes. If you are unsure of what exercise is best for you, or if you are concerned about safe levels of exercise, talk to your doctor or physiotherapist.

Tips for weight management

- *Be sensible. Don't adopt a stringent or poorly balanced diet plan. Short term, 'quick-fix' diets don't work in the long term.*

- *Establish a regular meal pattern – this will usually be breakfast, lunch and dinner. This helps you keep track of what and how much you eat and drink. Regular meals also help prevent hunger and keep energy levels up. If you are fairly active, include a healthy snack between meals.*

- *Limit fats and fatty foods. It may be a good idea to estimate your fat intake by using a 'Fat Counter' book. Refer to previous section on fats. Remember, fats are energy dense and are more easily deposited as body fat. Low-fat eating usually means low-kilojoule (calorie) eating.*

- *Limit alcohol. Alcohol contains considerable kilojoules (calories) and will contribute to being overweight, especially if consumed in conjunction with high-fat foods.*

- *Go easy on foods high in sugar, especially if they have little nutritional value. Small amounts of sugar such as jam on toast, or a little sugar in tea or coffee are acceptable. But limit soft drinks, cordials and fruit juices – look for the 'low-kilojoule (calorie)' or 'diet' alternatives.*

- *Incorporate regular exercise into your lifestyle.*

Most people find it difficult to lose weight – some more so than others. There are many factors involved including psychological (eating when depressed), social (excess alcohol), and medications (steroids). Try to address all these issues. Set realistic goals and be positive without being obsessive. Seek professional help if necessary.

5. if you drink alcohol, limit your intake

In small amounts, some alcoholic beverages are beneficial. In large quantities, however, none are safe.

Much of the reason that there has been so much interest in the possible benefits of alcohol, especially red wine, is what is known as the 'French paradox'. The French eat a lot of saturated fat, but have a relatively low rate of heart disease. Some experts attribute this to other aspects of their diet and lifestyle, others believe the effect is due to the red wine.

The benefit of alcohol, particularly in relation to heart disease, is that all types of alcohol increase HDL cholesterol i.e. the 'good' type of cholesterol in your blood. Wine, especially red wine, may have additional benefits. This is probably because it contains a higher amount of antioxidant vitamins (polyphenols) than most other alcoholic beverages. However, for those who dislike red wine, you can achieve an adequate intake of antioxidant vitamins by eating plenty of fruit and vegetables. Tea is also a good source of polyphenols.

You only need small amounts of alcohol to achieve these benefits. One to two standard alcoholic drinks (e.g. 1-2 small glasses of wine) a day is sufficient. Excessive intakes of alcohol can lead to high blood pressure, diabetes, liver problems, an increased risk of certain types of cancer, and can contribute to overweight.

6. choose low-salt foods and use salt sparingly

Salt is made up of sodium and chlorine. You need some sodium to maintain your body's proper fluid balance, however, most of us consume far more than we need. It is recommended that you aim to eat less than 2300 mg (100 mmol) of sodium per day. Most Australians consume at least twice this amount.

Where is the excess salt?
75% of the salt you eat comes from foods processed with salt and salt products, e.g. processed foods you buy at the supermarket and takeaway foods.

15% of salt comes from salt added at home when cooking and at the table, e.g. adding salt to vegetables when cooking.

Only 10% of salt comes from naturally occurring salt in foods, e.g. salt in fruits, vegetables and meat. Naturally occurring salt in foods is generally enough to meet your needs.

Eating too much salt may contribute to high blood pressure (hypertension) in some people. In turn, this increases the risk of heart disease, kidney disease and stroke. Too much salt can also contribute to many other diseases including osteoporosis and cancer. Salt will also aggravate fluid retention (oedema) which can occur in more severe heart disease when the heart cannot pump as effectively as normal.

How to eat less salt
- *Choose fresh foods where possible i.e. fresh fruit and vegetables, fresh meat and fish. These foods are naturally low in salt.*

- *If buying processed foods, try to choose those with less salt e.g labelled 'no-added-salt' or 'reduced-salt', especially foods eaten most often like bread, margarine and canned foods. A good guide is to check the nutrition information panel and look for products that are less than 120 mg sodium per 100 g of product. Unfortunately, in Australia, it is difficult to buy some products with a sodium content this low, in particular bread and cheese. Choose the best available, or talk to your dietitian about where to find low-salt versions.*

- *Use salt sparingly in cooking and at the table.*

- *Replace the taste. Many people will find if they do not replace the salt flavour with another flavour they will not enjoy their foods. Use any type and amount of fresh and dried herbs and spices as well as other flavourings such as lemon juice and vinegars as a replacement.*

- *Allow your taste buds time to adjust. The liking for salt is learned (babies do not like salt) and you need to unlearn this habit.*

7. eat only a moderate amount of sugars and foods containing added sugars

There is no direct link between sugar and heart disease. Sugar does not raise blood cholesterol levels nor cause diabetes. Most of the sugar in your diet is 'hidden' in processed foods such as soft drinks, cordials, fruit drinks, canned fruits in syrup, confectionery, biscuits, cakes, ice cream and jelly.

Moderate amounts of these foods are acceptable, but try to avoid those foods high in a combination of sugar and fat, such as biscuits, cakes, pastries, chocolate and some desserts.

For those keen to lose weight, it is best to choose the 'low-kilojoule (calorie)' or 'diet' versions e.g. 'diet' soft drinks and cordials. Artificial sweeteners such as Sugarine, Equal and Splenda are acceptable and safe.

8. encourage and support breast-feeding

For the first four to six months of life, babies are fed either by breast-feeding or a suitable milk-based formula. The benefits of breast-feeding, in particular the anti-infective components of breast milk, are well known. Mothers should be encouraged to breast-feed their baby if possible, and given adequate guidance and support as appropriate.

guidelines for specific nutrients

CALCIUM

Eat foods containing calcium. This is particularly important for girls and women.

Calcium is an essential mineral important for bone strength. An adequate calcium intake will help prevent osteoporosis (thinning of the bones). Dairy foods are the best food sources of calcium. Aim to eat at least two to three serves a day. The low-fat versions have just as much if not more calcium than their full-fat alternative. Calcium-fortified soy products and canned fish with edible bones are also good sources.

IRON

Eat foods containing iron. This applies particularly to girls, women, vegetarians and athletes.

Iron is an essential mineral important in the production of red blood cells which carry oxygen to all parts of the body. Iron also protects against infections. The best food sources of iron are lean meats, liver, poultry and seafood. Iron is found in smaller amounts in breads, breakfast cereals, vegetables, legumes, nuts and eggs.

firstcourses

Caribbean Gazpacho with Avocado Salsa

1/2 cup/90 g finely diced cucumber

1/2 cup/95 g finely diced pineapple

1/2 cup/95 g finely diced mango

1/4 red pepper, finely diced

2 plum tomatoes, finely diced

1 green onion, chopped

2 tablespoons chopped fresh mint

2 tablespoons chopped fresh coriander

1 cup/250 mL tomato or vegetable juice

1 cup/250 mL pineapple juice

1 teaspoon no-added-salt worcestershire sauce

tabasco sauce

AVOCADO SALSA

1 avocado, diced

1 tablespoon chopped fresh coriander

1 teaspoon lime juice

1   Place cucumber, pineapple, mango, red pepper, tomatoes, green onion, mint, coriander, tomato and pineapple juices, worcestershire sauce and tabasco sauce to taste in a glass bowl. Mix to combine. Cover. Refrigerate overnight or until cold.

2   **Salsa:** Place avocado, coriander and lime juice in a bowl. Mix to combine. Cover. Refrigerate until ready to use. Best used within a few days of making.

3   To serve, ladle soup into chilled bowls. Top with a spoonful of salsa.
Serves 4

876 kilojoules/211 Calories – per serve (with salsa)
14 g total fat; 3 g saturated fat; 238 mg sodium
343 kilojoules/81 Calories – per serve (without salsa)
less than 1 g total fat; nil saturated fat; 237 mg sodium

Spicy Tofu, Mushroom and Udon Soup

200 g firm tofu, diced

1 tablespoon reduced-salt soy sauce

1 tablespoon sherry or rice wine

10 g dried sliced mushrooms or 4 whole dried mushrooms

1 lemon myrtle or kaffir lime leaf

2-3 teaspoons olive or peanut oil

2 cm piece fresh ginger, thinly sliced

2 shallots, chopped or 1 green onion, sliced diagonally

6 fresh shiitake or flat mushrooms, thinly sliced

2 cups/80 g shredded English spinach or bok choy

250 g fresh udon noodles

4 cups/1 litre hot low-salt chicken stock (page 174) or dashi

1 tablespoon cider vinegar

1   Place tofu, soy sauce and sherry in a bowl. Toss to coat. Marinate for 10 minutes.

2   Place dried mushrooms and lemon myrtle leaf in a separate bowl. Pour over 1/2 cup/125 mL boiling water. Soak for 15 minutes or until mushrooms are tender.

3   Heat oil in a wok over a medium heat. Add ginger, shallots and fresh mushrooms. Stir-fry for 1-2 minutes. Add spinach and tofu with marinade. Stir-fry for 1 minute.

4   Add noodles, dried mushrooms with their soaking water, stock and vinegar. Bring to the boil. Remove lemon myrtle leaf. Discard. Serve immediately.
Serves 4

1656 kilojoules/394 Calories – per serve
5 g total fat; 2 g saturated fat; 401 mg sodium

Ingredient know-how: *Tofu, also known as soy bean curd, is an inexpensive, high-protein, low-fat ingredient often used in Asian cooking in place of meat and dairy products. Its unique silky texture and mild flavour make it ideal for taking on the flavour of other ingredients. For a vegetarian change, try marinating tofu in an Oriental sauce, then cook it on the barbecue or under the grill. Alternatively, cut tofu into cubes and stir-fry.*
For more information about lemon myrtle, see hint on page 56. You could also use 1/2 teaspoon ground lemon myrtle, but add it in the final stage of cooking.

Yellow Pepper Soup with Red Pepper Harissa

2 teaspoons olive oil

3 yellow peppers, diced

1 carrot, finely diced

1 small onion, diced

1 cup/200 g diced potato

2 cups/500 mL hot low-salt vegetable or chicken stock (pages 175 and 174)

2 teaspoons grated orange zest

juice of 1 orange

RED PEPPER HARISSA

2 red peppers, cut in half lengthwise, seeds removed

1 plum tomato, cut in half lengthwise, seeds removed

1 tablespoon red wine vinegar

2 teaspoons no-added-salt tomato paste

hot chilli sauce

freshly ground black pepper

1 **Harissa:** Preheat grill to hot. Using your hands, gently flatten red pepper and tomato halves and place, skin side up, on aluminium foil under grill. Cook until skins blacken. Set aside until cool enough to handle. Remove skins.

2 Place pepper and tomato flesh in a food processor. Add vinegar, tomato paste and hot chilli sauce and black pepper to taste. Purée. Set aside until ready to serve.

3 Heat oil in a nonstick saucepan over a low heat. Add yellow peppers, carrot and onion. Cook, stirring, for 10 minutes or until peppers are soft. Add potato and stock. Bring to simmering. Simmer for 20 minutes or until potato is soft. Cool slightly.

3 Transfer mixture to a food processor. Add orange zest and juice. Purée. Season with black pepper to taste. Return soup to a clean saucepan. Reheat.

4 To serve, ladle soup into warm bowls. Top with harissa.
Serves 4

596 kilojoules/141 Calories – per serve
3 g total fat; less than 1 g saturated fat; 80 mg sodium

Creamy Oyster Bisque

20 fresh oysters, shucked or 1 jar/about 20 oysters, drained, liquid reserved

low-salt fish or vegetable stock (pages 174 and 175)

1/2 cup/125 mL white wine

1 small white onion or 1/2 leek, diced

1 stalk celery, diced

2 cups/400 g diced peeled potato

1 tablespoon chopped fresh thyme or 1 teaspoon dried thyme

1/2 cup/125 mL low-fat milk

freshly ground black pepper

sprigs watercress or fresh parsley, optional

1 Measure liquid from oysters. Add stock to make up to 1 cup/250 mL.

2 Heat 2 tablespoons of the wine in a large saucepan over a low heat. Add onion and celery. Cook, stirring, for 4-5 minutes or until onion is transparent. Add potato and thyme. Stir in stock mixture and remaining wine. Bring to simmering. Simmer for 10-15 minutes or until potatoes are soft and most of the liquid is absorbed. Cool slightly.

3 Transfer mixture to a food processor or blender. Add half the oysters, the milk and black pepper to taste. Purée. Return mixture to a clean saucepan. Bring to the boil. Remove soup from heat. Stir in remaining oysters.

4 To serve, ladle soup into warm bowls and top with watercress or parsley sprigs, if desired.
Serves 4

616 kilojoules/147 Calories – per serve (using fresh oysters)
1 g total fat; less than 1 g saturated fat; 187 mg sodium

*Yellow Pepper Soup with
Red Pepper Harissa*

*Borsch with Cucumber
Yogurt (page 20)*

Creamy Oyster Bisque

19

Borsch with Cucumber Yogurt

1 tablespoon olive oil

1 onion, thinly sliced

1 clove garlic, crushed

1 cm piece fresh ginger, grated

1 tablespoon no-added-salt tomato paste

3 large beetroot, thinly sliced

1 large potato, thinly sliced

1 parsnip, thinly sliced

1 bay leaf

6 cups/1.5 litres low-salt chicken or vegetable stock
(pages 174 and 175)

2 tablespoons red wine vinegar

juice of 1 lemon or orange

freshly ground black pepper

CUCUMBER YOGURT

1/2 bunch/20 g fresh chives

1/4 cup/45 g finely diced cucumber

1 tablespoon chopped fresh dill

1 teaspoon lemon juice

1 cup/200 g thick low-fat natural yogurt

1   **Cucumber Yogurt:** Bring a saucepan of water to the boil. Blanch chives. Drain well. Place in a food processor. Add cucumber, dill and lemon juice. Process to make a paste. Transfer mixture to a bowl. Stir in yogurt. Cover. Refrigerate until ready to use.

2   Heat oil in a large, non-reactive saucepan over a medium heat. Add onion, garlic and ginger. Cook, stirring, for 5 minutes or until soft.

3   Stir in tomato paste. Cook for 1-2 minutes. Add beetroot, potato and parsnip. Cook, stirring, for 2-3 minutes. Add bay leaf, stock, vinegar and lemon juice. Bring to the boil. Reduce heat. Cover. Simmer for 30-40 minutes or until vegetables are soft. Season with black pepper to taste. Cool slightly.

4   Transfer mixture to a food processor or blender. Purée in batches. Return soup to a clean saucepan. Bring back to the boil. Check seasoning. Add more lemon juice if necessary.

5   To serve, ladle soup into warm bowls. Top with a spoonful of Cucumber Yogurt.

Serves 6

685 kilojoules/160 Calories – per serve
4 g total fat; less than 1 g saturated fat; 124 mg sodium

Thai Chicken Soup

2 cups/500 mL low-salt chicken stock (page 174)

2 kaffir lime or lemon myrtle leaves, optional

2 stalks fresh lemon grass or 2 teaspoons bottled lemon grass

1 bunch/150 g fresh coriander with roots

5 thin slices fresh galangal or ginger

1 skinless chicken breast fillet, cut into thin strips

2 shallots, sliced

2 fresh bird's eye chillies or to taste

pinch sugar

2 tablespoons rice wine (mirin) or sherry

juice of 1 lime

1   Place stock and lime leaves in a large saucepan. Bring to the boil.

2   Meanwhile, remove outer layers from lemon grass. Chop. Cut the roots from two of the coriander plants. Chop. Remove leaves from remaining coriander. Set aside.

3   Place lemon grass, coriander roots and galangal in a mortar. Bruise with a pestle. Alternatively, place ingredients in a plastic food bag. Bruise with a rolling pin.

4   Stir lemon grass mixture into stock. Bring to simmering. Simmer for 2-3 minutes. Add chicken and shallots. Simmer for 5-6 minutes or until chicken is cooked.

5   Place reserved coriander leaves, chillies, sugar, fish sauce and lime juice in a small bowl. Mix to combine.

6   To serve, divide mixture between warm soup bowls. Ladle over soup. Mix gently to combine. For a main meal, serve with steamed jasmine rice.

Serves 2

910 kilojoules/211 Calories – per serve
3 g total fat; 1 g saturated fat; 123 mg sodium

Blinis with Herbed Yogurt Cheese

½ quantity Yogurt Cheese (page 176), flavoured with 1 tablespoon chopped fresh dill and 1 tablespoon chopped fresh mint

BLINIS

1 teaspoon dry yeast

1 teaspoon sugar

1½ cups/375 mL low-fat milk, warmed

1 cup/130 g buckwheat flour

½ cup/125 g plain flour

1 egg white

freshly ground black pepper

1   **Blinis:** Place yeast, sugar and ½ cup/125 mL of the milk in a small bowl. Stand for 5 minutes or until frothy.

2   Place buckwheat and plain flours in a large bowl. Mix to combine. Make a well in the centre. Pour yeast mixture and remaining milk into well. Mix until just combined.

3   Place egg white in a separate clean bowl. Beat until soft peaks form. Fold egg mixture into batter. Season with black pepper to taste.

4   Heat a nonstick frying pan over a medium heat. Lightly spray or brush with unsaturated oil. Place tablespoons of mixture in pan – you should be able to cook 5-6 blinis at a time in a 20-23 cm frying pan. Cook for 1-2 minutes or until bubbles appear on the surface. Turn over. Cook second side for 30 seconds or until golden. Place on absorbent kitchen paper. Keep warm in a low oven while cooking the remaining mixture.

5   Serve blinis warm or cold topped with a spoonful of Yogurt Cheese and a low-fat topping of your choice, if desired – shown here topped with semi-dried tomatoes.

Makes 20

277 kilojoules/67 Calories – per blini (with yogurt cheese)
less than 1 g total fat; less than 1 g saturated fat; 35 mg sodium
210 kilojoules/51 Calories – per blini (without yogurt cheese)
less than 1 g total fat; less than 1 g saturated fat; 14 mg sodium

Curried Sweet Potato Soup

2 teaspoons canola oil

½ carrot, diced

½ onion, diced

1 stalk celery, diced

1 clove garlic, crushed

2 teaspoons curry powder

½ teaspoon cumin seeds

½ teaspoon yellow mustard seeds

2 tablespoons chopped fresh coriander

4 cups/1 litre low-salt vegetable stock (page 175)

½ cup/125 mL beer or stout

1 tablespoon honey

500 g orange sweet potato, chopped

½ teaspoon ground cinnamon

1 sugar banana, chopped, optional

lime wedges

LIME YOGURT

½ cup/100 g low-fat natural yogurt

2 teaspoons finely grated lime zest

2 teaspoons lime juice

1   Heat oil in a saucepan over a medium heat. Add carrot, onion, celery and garlic. Cook, stirring, for 3 minutes. Stir in curry powder and cumin and mustard seeds. Cook until the mustard seeds start to pop.

2   Add coriander, stock, beer and honey. Bring to the boil. Add sweet potato, cinnamon and banana. Simmer, stirring occasionally, until sweet potato is soft. Cool slightly.

3   Transfer mixture to a food processor or blender. Purée in batches. Return mixture to a clean saucepan. Reheat.

4   **Lime Yogurt:** Place yogurt and lime zest and juice in a small bowl. Mix to combine.

5   To serve, ladle soup into warm bowls. Top with a spoonful of Lime Yogurt. Serve with lime wedges.

Serves 6

622 kilojoules/146 Calories – per serve
2 g total fat; less than 1 g saturated fat; 67 mg sodium

Author's note: *The banana creates a unique flavour, one that I love but you may not. The soup is still divine without it.*

Blinis with Herbed Yogurt Cheese

Pork Apple Parcels

800-900 g lean pork schnitzel, trimmed of visible fat, pounded until very thin

2 granny smith, royal gala or braeburn apples, chopped

^{1}/$_2$ cup/60 g sultanas

juice of ^{1}/$_2$ lemon

^{1}/$_2$ cup/125 mL plum sauce

^{1}/$_2$ cup/125 mL apple juice

1 tablespoon reduced-salt soy sauce

1 tablespoon honey

1   Preheat oven to 180°C.

2   Cut pork into 10 cm squares. Set aside.

3   Place apples, sultanas and lemon juice in a bowl. Mix to combine. Spread each pork square with plum sauce to within 2 cm of the edges. Place a small mound of the apple mixture in the centre. Roll up to form a parcel. Tie with cooking string. Place in a casserole dish.

4   Combine apple juice, soy sauce and honey. Pour over pork parcels. Cover loosely with aluminium foil. Bake for 20-25 minutes or until pork is browned and tender. Remove parcels from casserole dish.

5   Stir 2 tablespoons plum sauce into cooking juices. Serve with parcels for dipping.

Makes 12 parcels

745 kilojoules/177 Calories – per parcel
3 g total fat; 1 g saturated fat; 197 mg sodium

Moroccan Lemon Chicken Shish Kebabs

500 g skinless chicken breast fillets, trimmed of visible fat, cut into 2 cm cubes

1 quantity Red Pepper Harissa (see Yellow Pepper Soup page 18), optional

MOROCCAN LEMON MARINADE

1 tablespoon chopped fresh parsley

1 tablespoon fresh rosemary leaves or 2 teaspoons dried rosemary

2 teaspoons fresh thyme or 1 teaspoon dried thyme

1 clove garlic, crushed

1 teaspoon crushed black peppercorns

grated zest and juice of 1 lemon or 1 preserved lemon

1 tablespoon olive oil

1   **Marinade:** Place parsley, rosemary, thyme, garlic, black pepper, lemon juice and zest and oil in a non-reactive bowl. Add chicken. Toss to combine. Cover. Marinate in the refrigerator for at least 30 minutes.

2   Preheat barbecue or grill to a high heat. If using bamboo skewers, soak in cold water for at least 20 minutes.

3   Thread chicken onto skewers. Place on barbecue grill or under grill. Cook, brushing frequently with marinade and turning, for 6-10 minutes or until chicken is cooked. Serve with Red Pepper Harissa for dipping.

Makes 8 kebabs

498 kilojoules/117 Calories – per kebab (with harissa)
4 g total fat; 1 g saturated fat; 66 mg sodium
401 kilojoules/95 Calories – per kebab (without harissa)
4 g total fat; 1 g saturated fat; 35 mg sodium

Curried Sweet Potato Soup
(page 22)

Moroccan Lemon Chicken
Shish Kebabs

Pork Apple Parcels

25

Teriyaki Calamari Skewers

2 large calamari (squid) tubes, cleaned, cut into 5 mm thick rings

TERIYAKI SAUCE

1 shallot, thinly sliced

1 teaspoon minced fresh ginger

1/4 cup/60 mL rice wine vinegar or sherry

2 tablespoons reduced-salt soy sauce

1 teaspoon honey

2 tablespoons lime or lemon juice

1 teaspoon sesame oil

1   Soak 24 small or 8 large bamboo skewers in cold water for at least 20 minutes.

2   Preheat a barbecue or grill to a high heat.

3   Cut each calamari ring in half. Thread strips onto bamboo skewers in an 'S' shape – use 1 strip on small skewers and 3 strips on large skewers.

4   Place skewers on barbecue or under grill. Cook, turning several times, for 1-2 minutes or until calamari is just cooked.

5   **Teriyaki Sauce:** Place shallot, ginger, vinegar, soy sauce, honey and 1 tablespoon lime juice in a small saucepan over medium heat. Heat. Stir in sesame oil and remaining lime juice. Serve with skewers. If serving as a light meal, accompany with a tossed green salad. The skewers are delicious warm or cold.

**Makes 24 small skewers for a first course or
8 large skewers for a light meal – allow 2 skewers per serve**

90 kilojoules/21 Calories – per small skewer
less than 1 g total fat; less than 1 g saturated fat; 104 mg sodium
271 kilojoules/64 Calories – per large skewer
1 g total fat; less than 1 g saturated fat; 311 mg sodium

Oyster Spring Rolls

2 tablespoons grated fresh ginger or shredded pickled ginger

1 tablespoon chopped fresh coriander or dill

1 tablespoon finely chopped chives or green onions

1 teaspoon lime or lemon juice

5 sheets spring roll pastry or 20 wonton wraps

20 fresh oysters, shucked or 1 jar/about 20 oysters, drained

DIPPING SAUCE

1 green onion, sliced diagonally

2 tablespoons rice wine vinegar

2 tablespoons reduced-salt soy sauce

1 tablespoon lime or lemon juice

1   Preheat oven to 180°C. Lightly spray or brush a baking tray with unsaturated oil.

2   **Sauce:** Place green onion, vinegar, soy sauce and lime juice in a small serving bowl. Mix to combine. Set aside.

3   Place ginger, coriander, chives and lime juice in a small bowl. Mix to combine.

4   Cut each sheet of spring roll pastry into four squares. Place an oyster on the centre of each square. Top with a little of the ginger mixture. Brush edges with water. Fold in sides. Roll up.

5   Place rolls, seam side down, on prepared baking tray. Bake for 10-12 minutes or until pastry is crisp and golden. Serve with Dipping Sauce.

Makes 20 mini spring rolls

76 kilojoules/18 Calories – per roll (using fresh oysters)
less than 1 g total fat; less than 1 g saturated fat; 127 mg sodium

Author's note: *These spring rolls can also be steamed or pan-fried. Filo pastry can be used instead of the spring roll pastry. Bake in the same way. For something different, make them with prawns, scallops, tofu or vegetables such as mushrooms and Chinese cabbage.*
When working with spring roll or filo pastry, keep the pastry you are not working with covered with a damp cloth. This prevents it from drying out.

Olive Scones with Thyme Cured Beef

chutney of your choice

fresh thyme sprigs

THYME CURED BEEF

³/₄ cup/185 g sugar

¹/₂ cup/125 g salt

3 tablespoons crushed black peppercorns

1 large bunch/50 g fresh thyme, leaves only

200 g lean beef fillet, trimmed of visible fat

OLIVE SCONES

2 cups/250 g plain flour

2 teaspoons baking powder

¹/₄ cup/45 g black olives, rinsed and drained, chopped

1 tablespoon chopped fresh basil

freshly ground black pepper

1 cup/250 mL buttermilk

1 tablespoon dijon mustard

1   **Curing beef:** Place sugar, salt, peppercorns and thyme leaves on a large plate. Roll beef in mixture several times to coat and form a crust. Place beef on a rack set in a shallow dish. Cover. Refrigerate for 24 hours – check from time to time that the crust is still encasing the meat as the juices that are released during marinating may loosen it.

2   When ready, using absorbent kitchen paper, thoroughly wipe away all of the herb crust. Using a very sharp knife, cut beef across the grain into paper-thin slices – this is easier to do if you place the fillet in the freezer for 10 minutes before slicing. Place slices on a plate. Cover. Refrigerate until ready to use.

3   **Scones:** Preheat oven to 210°C. Lightly spray or brush a baking tray with unsaturated oil. Set aside.

4   Sift flour and baking powder together into a large bowl. Add olives, basil and black pepper to taste. Mix to combine. Make a well in the centre. Place milk and mustard in a small bowl. Whisk to combine. Pour into well in flour mixture. Mix quickly to make a soft dough. Turn dough onto a lightly floured surface. Knead briefly until smooth.

5   Press mixture or roll out to form a 2 cm thick rectangle. Using a 3 cm scone cutter, cut out scones. Place with sides just touching on prepared baking tray. Bake for 10-12 minutes or until scones are well risen and golden. Transfer to a wire rack. Cool slightly.

6   To serve, split scones and spread with a little chutney. Top with a small mound of beef and a thyme sprig.

Makes 24 scones or 48 open-faced canapés

84 kilojoules/21 Calories – per canapé (without chutney)
less than 1 g total fat; less than 1 g saturated fat; 3 mg sodium

Author's note: *The curing process may look complicated, but it really is quite simple and produces such a tender and succulent result, no one will believe you did it yourself. You may get a shock at the amount of sugar and salt in this recipe, but don't be alarmed. You wipe it all off once the curing is over and it has drawn the juices out of the beef. If you don't want to bother with the process of curing the beef, just use shaved lean beef or lamb. The idea for this cured beef was given to me by a friend and truly inspired American chef, Randal St Clair, who is currently Executive Chef at my favourite Sydney hotel, The Observatory.*

Gravlax Spirals

½ cup/125 g reduced-fat ricotta cheese

3 tablespoons chopped fresh dill

½ cup/100 g low-fat natural yogurt

2 slices lavash bread

¼ cup/60 mL honey mustard

100 g gravlax, smoked salmon or smoked ocean trout

lemon juice

freshly ground black pepper

1   Place ricotta cheese, dill and yogurt in bowl. Mix to combine. Set aside.

2   Spread lavash bread with mustard. Top with salmon. Spread with ricotta mixture – leave 10 cm at one short end uncovered. Sprinkle with lemon juice and black pepper to taste.

3   Starting at the covered short end, roll up firmly. Wrap in plastic food wrap. Refrigerate for several hours or until ready to serve.

4   To serve, cut rolls into 2 cm thick slices. Arrange attractively on a serving platter.

Makes 20 pieces

173 kilojoules/41 Calories – per piece
1 g total fat; less than 1 g saturated fat; 127 mg sodium

Baked Ricotta Mushrooms

10 mushroom caps, stems removed

1 tablespoon grated parmesan cheese

1 tablespoon dried breadcrumbs

RICOTTA AND HERB FILLING

½ cup/125 g reduced-fat fresh ricotta cheese

3 sun-dried tomatoes, soaked in warm water until soft, chopped

1 tablespoon finely diced red onion

1 tablespoon chopped fresh basil

1 tablespoon snipped fresh chives

1 teaspoon lemon juice

freshly ground black pepper

1   Preheat oven to 180°C. Line a baking tray with nonstick baking paper. Set aside.

2   **Filling:** Place ricotta cheese, tomatoes, onion, basil, chives, lemon juice and black pepper to taste in a bowl. Mix to combine.

3   Spoon filling into mushrooms. Place on prepared baking tray. Combine parmesan cheese and breadcrumbs. Sprinkle over mushrooms. Bake for 10-15 minutes or until filling is set and top golden.

Makes 10

129 kilojoules/31 Calories – per mushroom
1 g total fat; 1 g saturated fat; 46 mg sodium

lightmeals

Roast Beet and Smoked Trout Salad

6-8 baby beetroot, trimmed

3 tablespoons red wine vinegar or rice vinegar

1 large or 2 small smoked rainbow or river trout

1 tablespoon fresh lemon juice

freshly ground black pepper

2 tablespoons fresh dill leaves

1 teaspoon dijon or dill mustard

1 tablespoon virgin olive oil

6 cups/225 g mixed salad greens

1   Preheat oven to 180°C. Wrap each beetroot in aluminium foil. Bake for 20 minutes or until tender. Cool to warm. Peel. Cut into quarters. Place in a bowl. Add 1 tablespoon of the vinegar. Toss. Set aside.

2   Remove skin from trout and discard. Remove flesh in large flakes. Place in a separate bowl. Add half the lemon juice and black pepper to taste. Toss gently. Set aside.

3   Place remaining vinegar and lemon juice, dill, mustard and oil in a small bowl. Whisk to combine.

4   To serve, line a large serving platter with salad greens. Arrange beetroot and trout attractively on top. Drizzle with dressing.
Serves 6

543 kilojoules/140 Calories – per serve
6 g total fat; 1 g saturated fat; 70 mg sodium

Niçoise Tuna Baguettes

4 small baguettes or 1 long baguette, cut into 4 pieces

200 g canned tuna in springwater, drained and flaked

200 g green beans, blanched

1 red pepper, cut into strips

4 plum tomatoes, cut into thick slices

2 hard-boiled eggs, sliced

1/2 red onion, thinly sliced

2 tablespoons sliced black olives, rinsed and drained

4 leaves cos or butter lettuce

MUSTARD AND YOGURT DRESSING

4 canned anchovy fillets, rinsed and drained

1 tablespoon low-fat natural yogurt

1 teaspoon wholegrain mustard

2 tablespoons red wine vinegar

2 teaspoons olive oil

1   Preheat oven to 180°C. Wrap baguettes in aluminium foil. Bake for 10 minutes or until crisp and warm.

2   **Dressing:** Place anchovies, yogurt, mustard, vinegar and oil in a blender. Purée.

3   Place tuna, beans, red pepper, tomatoes, eggs, onion and olives in a bowl. Pour over dressing. Toss to combine.

4   Split warm baguettes, taking care not to cut all the way through. Place a lettuce leaf on one side. Top with filling and close baguette. Serve immediately.
Makes 4 baguettes

1049 kilojoules/251 Calories – per serve
8 g total fat; 2 g saturated fat; 575 mg sodium

Niçoise Tuna Baguettes
Rice, Vegetable and Feta Strata (page 36)

Rice, Vegetable and Feta Strata

2 cups/200 g thinly sliced mixed vegetables of your choice – I like to use a combination of zucchini (courgettes), broccoli and mushrooms

3/4 cup/90 g crumbled reduced-fat and -salt feta cheese

1 cup/210 g wild and brown rice blend, cooked – you should have about 2 1/2 cups of cooked rice

2 tablespoons chopped fresh herbs (e.g. parsley, basil, chives or coriander)

1/4 cup/60 mL buttermilk or low-fat milk

1 egg

2 egg whites

1 teaspoon ground nutmeg

1 teaspoon dried oregano

freshly ground black pepper

2 tablespoons pine nuts or pepitas (pumpkin seeds), optional

1   Preheat oven to 190°C. Lightly spray or brush a 25 cm pie or quiche dish with unsaturated oil.

2   Steam or microwave vegetables until tender crisp. Place in a bowl. Cool slightly. Add half the cheese. Toss to combine. Place rice, fresh herbs and remaining cheese in a separate bowl. Mix to combine.

3   Press rice mixture into base of prepared dish. Top with vegetable mixture.

4   Place milk, egg, egg whites, nutmeg, oregano and black pepper to taste in a bowl. Whisk to combine. Carefully pour over vegetables. Scatter with pine nuts.

5   Bake for 40-45 minutes or until golden and set. Delicious served hot or warm with a green salad.

Makes 8 slices

754 kilojoules/182 Calories – per slice
7 g total fat; 2 g saturated fat; 70 mg sodium

Tuscan Vegetable Terrine

1 bunch/180 g rocket
Italian bread

VEGETABLE TERRINE

300 g pumpkin, peeled

16 plum tomatoes

400 g bocconcini cheese, well-drained

1 bunch/50 g fresh basil

freshly ground black pepper

MUSTARD AND BALSAMIC DRESSING

1 teaspoon wholegrain mustard

2 tablespoons balsamic vinegar

2 tablespoons olive oil

1   Preheat oven to 180°C. Line a terrine or loaf dish with plastic food wrap, leaving enough wrap overhanging the sides to cover top of terrine. Set aside.

2   **Terrine:** Cut pumpkin into 1 cm thick slices to fit shape of terrine – there should be enough for a single layer in the terrine. Lightly spray or brush slices with olive oil. Place on a baking tray. Bake for 20-30 minutes or until pumpkin is cooked, but still firm. Cool.

3   Cut tomatoes in half lengthwise. Remove seeds and press gently with hands to flatten. Cut cheese into 6 mm thick slices.

4   Layer the ingredients in the terrine in the following order – tomatoes, basil leaves, cheese, tomatoes, basil leaves, cheese, pumpkin, basil leaves, tomatoes, cheese, basil leaves, tomatoes and finally cheese. The overall effect should be layers of tomatoes, basil and cheese with a layer of pumpkin in the centre. When layering, place the tomatoes skin side down and season each tomato layer with a little black pepper. Cover terrine with the overhanging plastic wrap. Weigh down. Refrigerate overnight.

5   **Dressing:** Place mustard, vinegar and oil in a screwtop jar. Shake well to combine. Set aside until ready to use.

6   To serve, using the plastic wrap, carefully lift terrine from dish. Cut into thick slices. Line serving plates with rocket leaves. Place a slice of terrine on top. Drizzle with dressing. Accompany with Italian bread.

Serves 8-10

1332 kilojoules/321 Calories – per serve
14 g total fat; 6 g saturated fat; 522 mg sodium

Tuscan Vegetable Terrine

Salmon and Potato Lasagne

1 teaspoon olive oil

1 onion, diced

2 stalks celery, diced

1 tablespoon no-added-salt tomato paste

210 g canned no-added-salt red or pink salmon, rinsed, drained and roughly mashed – don't remove the bones, they're full of calcium

1 tablespoon chopped fresh tarragon or 1 teaspoon dried tarragon

300 mL low-fat milk

3 eggs, lightly beaten

2 egg whites, lightly beaten

juice of $\frac{1}{2}$ lemon

freshly ground black pepper

4 large potatoes, thinly sliced

4 cups/200 g firmly packed English spinach leaves, blanched and squeezed to remove excess moisture

BREADCRUMB AND PARMESAN TOPPING

$\frac{1}{2}$ cup/30 g breadcrumbs, made from stale bread

2 tablespoons chopped fresh parsley

1 tablespoon grated parmesan cheese

1 Preheat oven to 180°C. Lightly spray or brush a large flat casserole dish with unsaturated oil.

2 Heat oil in a nonstick frying pan over a medium heat. Add onion and celery. Cook, stirring, for 3-4 minutes or until soft. Stir in tomato paste. Cook for 3-4 minutes or until it becomes deep red and develops a rich aroma. Transfer mixture to a large bowl. Cool.

3 **Topping:** Place breadcrumbs, parsley and parmesan cheese in a small bowl. Mix to combine. Set aside.

4 Add salmon, tarragon, milk, eggs, egg whites, lemon juice and black pepper to taste to onion mixture. Mix to combine. Arrange half the potatoes over the base of the prepared dish. Pour over salmon mixture. Top with spinach. Cover with remaining potatoes. Sprinkle with topping. Bake for 1 hour or until the potatoes are tender and mixture is set.

Serves 4

1184 kilojoules/284 Calories – per serve
7 g total fat; 2 g saturated fat; 254 mg sodium

White Bean Nachos with Roast Tomato Salsa

Homemade Corn Chips (page 176) – made using 8 corn or wheat tortillas

FRIED WHITE BEANS

2 teaspoons olive oil

$\frac{1}{2}$ carrot, finely diced

2 green onions or 1 small white onion, finely chopped

1 clove garlic, crushed

1 teaspoon ground cumin

1 teaspoon ground coriander

450 g cooked or canned white beans (e.g. cannellini or lima), rinsed and drained

$\frac{1}{2}$ cup/125 mL low-salt chicken stock

1 tablespoon lemon juice

3 tablespoons chopped fresh coriander

1 quantity Roasted Chilli Tomato Salsa (page 170) or $\frac{1}{2}$ cup/125 mL purchased no-added-salt taco sauce

1 Make corn chips as directed in recipe.

2 **Fried beans:** Heat oil in a nonstick frying pan over a medium heat. Add carrot, onions and garlic. Cook, stirring, for 2-3 minutes or until soft. Stir in cumin and ground coriander. Cook for 1 minute or until fragrant.

3 Add beans and stock. Bring to simmering. Simmer, stirring and roughly mashing the beans occasionally, for 10 minutes or until mixture reduces and thickens – if the mixture becomes too thick, add a little more stock. Stir in lemon juice and fresh coriander.

4 To serve, place bean mixture and salsa in separate bowls on a serving platter. Surround with corn chips. Alternatively, line a serving platter with corn chips. Spoon bean mixture into the centre. Top with salsa.

Serves 4

550 kilojoules/132 Calories – per serve (using fresh cooked beans)
3 g total fat; less than 1 g saturated fat; 39 mg sodium

Cook's tip: *For a smooth bean mixture, place the cooked mixture in a food processor and purée, then reheat prior to serving.*

Salmon and Potato Lasagne

*White Bean Nachos with
Roast Tomato Salsa*

*Roast Vegetable Pide with
Dill Sauce (page 40)*

39

Roast Vegetable Pide With Dill Sauce

2 zucchini (courgettes), cut into thick slices

4 yellow baby squash, cut into quarters

1 red pepper, diced

1 green or yellow pepper, diced

1 large red onion, diced

6 cherry tomatoes, halved

1 tablespoon olive oil

1 large pide (Turkish bread), cut into 4 pieces, split

4 tablespoons chopped fresh basil

1 tablespoon dijon or wholegrain mustard

1 tablespoon balsamic vinegar

freshly ground black pepper

mixed salad greens

DILL SAUCE

2 tablespoons crumbled reduced-fat and -salt feta cheese

$^1/_2$ cup/100 g low-fat natural yogurt

1 tablespoon lemon juice

2 tablespoons chopped fresh dill or parsley

1   Preheat oven to 200°C. Place zucchini, squash, red and green peppers, onion, tomatoes and olive oil in a bowl. Toss to coat. Lightly spray or brush a baking dish with unsaturated oil. Spread vegetable mixture over base of dish. Bake for 25-30 minutes or until vegetables are tender and golden.

2   **Sauce:** Meanwhile, place cheese, yogurt and lemon juice in a food processor. Process until smooth. Transfer to a bowl. Stir in dill. Cover. Refrigerate until ready to serve.

3   Wrap bread in aluminium foil. Place in oven 5-7 minutes before the vegetables are completely cooked, to warm. Place basil, mustard and vinegar in a small bowl. Mix to combine. Add to vegetable mixture. Toss to combine.

4   Top the base of each piece of pide bread with salad greens. Spoon over vegetable mixture. Drizzle with a little sauce and cover with top piece of bread.
Serves 4

1159 kilojoules/278 Calories – per serve
9 g total fat; 2 g saturated fat; 334 mg sodium

Mixed Mushroom and Goat's Cheese Strudel

1 teaspoon extra virgin olive oil

2 green onions, finely diced

2 cloves garlic, crushed

500 g mixed mushrooms of your choice (e.g. shiitake, Swiss or oyster), diced

100 mL white wine

1 teaspoon lemon juice

75 g reduced-fat and -salt goat's cheese, crumbled

3 tablespoons chopped fresh mixed herbs (e.g. sage, thyme, oregano, rosemary)

8 sheets filo pastry

freshly ground black pepper

DRIED MUSHROOM AND HERB BROTH (OPTIONAL)

2 cups/500 mL water

1 cup/20 g dried mushrooms

2 tablespoons no-added-salt tomato paste

1 tablespoon chopped fresh herbs (e.g. parsley, basil, chives or coriander)

1 tablespoon sherry

1   Heat oil in a frying pan over a low heat. Add onions and garlic. Cook, stirring, for 2-3 minutes or until soft and translucent. Add mushrooms. Cook, stirring occasionally, for 5-8 minutes or until juices evaporate. Stir in wine and lemon juice. Cook, stirring occasionally, until liquid is absorbed. Cool.

2   Preheat oven to 180°C. Lightly spray or brush a baking tray with olive oil or line with nonstick baking paper. Set aside.

3   Stir cheese and fresh herbs into mushroom mixture. Lay 2 sheets of filo pastry on a clean, dry work surface. Lightly spray or brush with olive oil and season with black pepper. Place 2 more sheets on top. Place half the mushroom mixture along the long edge leaving a 3 cm border at each end. Fold in ends. Roll up tightly. Place seam down on prepared baking tray. Repeat with remaining filo and mushroom mixture to make a second strudel. Using a sharp knife, make slashes in the top of each strudel to mark slices. Bake for 10-12 minutes or until golden.

4   **Broth:** Place water in a saucepan. Bring to the boil. Add mushrooms, tomato paste, herbs and sherry. Boil until mushrooms are tender and mixture starts to thicken.

5   Cut strudels where marked. Serve with or without broth.
Makes 2 strudels – each cuts into 4 thick slices

446 kilojoules/107 Calories – per slice (with broth)
3 g total fat; 1 g saturated fat; 138 mg sodium
412 kilojoules/98 Calories – per slice (without broth)
2 g total fat; 1 g saturated fat; 134 mg sodium

Mixed Mushroom and Goat's Cheese Strudel

Baked Chicken and Vegetable Lavash Rolls

2 tablespoons no-added-salt peanut butter

3 tablespoons no-added-salt tomato paste

$^1/_2$ teaspoon sweet chilli sauce or to taste

4 slices lavash bread

CHICKEN AND VEGETABLE FILLING

1 cup/180 g shredded cooked chicken

1 cup/125 g grated pumpkin

1 cup/135 g grated zucchini (courgettes)

1 cup/75 g finely shredded cabbage or spinach

1 cup/90 g sliced mushrooms

1 teaspoon ground cumin

1 teaspoon ground coriander

2 tablespoons chopped fresh coriander

1 tablespoon sesame seeds, toasted

1   Preheat oven to 190°C. Lightly spray or brush a shallow baking dish with unsaturated oil or line with nonstick baking paper.

2   Place peanut butter, tomato paste and chilli sauce to taste in a small bowl. Mix to combine. Spread over one side of each piece of lavash bread, leaving a 2 cm border.

3   **Filling:** Place chicken, pumpkin, zucchini, cabbage, mushrooms, cumin, ground and fresh coriander and sesame seeds in a bowl. Mix to combine. Place one-quarter of the filling in a band near one short end of each piece of bread, leaving 3 cm at top and bottom. Fold in sides. Starting at the filling end, roll up firmly. Place rolls, seam side down, in prepared baking dish. Bake for 15 minutes or until golden. Delicious served with Roasted Chilli Tomato Salsa or Cucumber Yogurt Sauce (pages 170 and 172).

Makes 4 rolls

1222 kilojoules/294 Calories – per roll
10 g total fat; 2 g saturated fat; 329 mg sodium

Cook's tip: *Lavash bread goes back many thousands of years to Biblical times. It is very thin (about the same as a tortilla), usually has no added fats or yeast and is very versatile. Similar breads can be found called Mountain and Sorj Bread or you could also use square tortillas. I've given you two ideas but the scope is only as limited as your own imagination.*

Baked Pastrami and Tomato Lavash Rolls

$^1/_2$ cup/125 g reduced-fat ricotta cheese

2 tablespoons dijon mustard

1 tablespoon shredded fresh basil

4 slices lavash bread

8 slices lean pastrami or lean roast beef

PASTRAMI AND TOMATO FILLING

1 cup/125 g cooked or canned butter beans or other beans of your choice, rinsed and drained

4 plum tomatoes, sliced

3 small balls bocconcini cheese, thinly sliced

1 cup/45 g shredded radicchio

2 green onions, sliced

2 tablespoons sliced olives, rinsed and drained

1   Preheat oven to 190°C. Lightly spray or brush a shallow baking dish with unsaturated oil or line with nonstick baking paper.

2   Place ricotta cheese, mustard and basil in a small bowl. Mix to combine. Spread over one side of each piece of lavash bread, leaving a 2 cm border. Top each piece of bread with 2 slices of pastrami.

3   **Filling:** Place beans, tomatoes, bocconcini, radicchio, onions and olives in a bowl. Toss to combine. Place one-quarter of the filling in a band near one short end of each piece of bread, leaving 3 cm at top and bottom. Fold in sides. Starting at the filling end, roll up firmly. Place rolls, seam side down, in prepared baking dish. Bake for 15 minutes or until golden. Delicious served with Roasted Chilli Tomato Salsa or Cucumber Yogurt Sauce (pages 170 and 172).

Makes 4 rolls

1518 kilojoules/364 Calories – per roll (made with pastrami, using fresh cooked beans)
13 g total fat; 5 g saturated fat; 938 mg sodium
1304 kilojoules/313 Calories – per roll (made with roast beef, using fresh cooked beans)
10 g total fat; 5 g saturated fat; 438 mg sodium

Corn and Wild Rice Fritters with Tomato

3 large vine ripened tomatoes, cut into thick slices

2 cups/75 g rocket leaves

CORN AND WILD RICE FRITTERS

2 cobs sweet corn, kernels removed

1 cup/150 g cooked wild rice or wild rice blend

1 tablespoon chopped fresh parsley

1 tablespoon snipped fresh chives

2 teaspoons fresh rosemary leaves, chopped

2 eggs, lightly beaten

2 egg whites, lightly beaten

freshly ground black pepper

1 **Fritters:** Heat a large nonstick frying pan over a high heat. Lightly spray or brush with unsaturated oil. Add sweet corn kernels. Cook, stirring, for 2-3 minutes or until they start to brown. Transfer to a large bowl. Add rice, parsley, chives, rosemary, eggs, egg whites and black pepper to taste. Mix to combine.

2 Lightly spray or brush frying pan with unsaturated oil. Place 1/2 cup/125 mL of mixture in pan – allow room between each fritter for spreading. Cook for 2-3 minutes each side or until crisp and golden. Remove fritters from pan. Place on absorbent kitchen paper and keep warm while cooking remaining mixture.

3 Meanwhile, preheat grill to a high heat. Place tomatoes on aluminium foil. Season with black pepper to taste. Cook under grill for 5 minutes or until hot. To serve, top each fritter with a few rocket leaves and some tomato slices.

Makes 6 fritters

718 kilojoules/173 Calories – per serve
2 g total fat; 1 g saturated fat; 45 mg sodium

Cook's tip: *When cooking wild rice, to achieve beautiful plump grains with a curly appearance, place rice in cold water, bring to the boil and boil for 5 minutes. Turn off heat, cover and steam for 20-30 minutes. Bring to the boil again and cook for 15 minutes longer or until rice is tender.*

Stir-fried Tortilla Wrap

4 large corn or flour tortillas

1 tablespoon reduced-salt soy sauce

1 tablespoon low-salt chicken stock (page 174) or water

2 teaspoons honey

1 teaspoon hoisin sauce

1 teaspoon unsaturated oil

3 green onions, cut into 3 cm long pieces

2 cm piece fresh ginger, chopped

300 g lean steak (e.g. rump, topside, blade or round), trimmed of visible fat, cut into thin strips

1 carrot, cut into long strips

1 green pepper, cut into long strips

1/2 daikon (white radish) or 1 stalk celery, cut into long strips

6-8 green beans or fresh asparagus spears, halved lengthwise

1 cup/45 g shredded radicchio or red cabbage

1 cup/90 g snow pea (mangetout) shoots

low-fat natural yogurt, optional

2 tablespoons sesame seeds, toasted

1 Preheat oven to 180°C. Wrap tortillas in aluminium foil. Warm in oven for 5 minutes – do not heat too long or tortillas become crisp. Alternatively, wrap in a clean cloth and heat in the microwave on HIGH (100%) for 30-60 seconds.

2 Place soy sauce, stock, honey and hoisin sauce in a small bowl. Mix to combine. Set aside.

3 Heat oil in a wok or nonstick frying pan over a medium heat. Add onions and ginger. Stir-fry for 1 minute. Add beef. Stir-fry for 3-4 minutes or until it changes colour. Add carrot, green pepper, daikon and beans. Stir-fry for 2-3 minutes.

4 Add radicchio, snow pea shoots and soy sauce mixture. Toss. Cover. Turn off heat. Steam for 1-2 minutes.

5 Spread tortillas with yogurt. Place one-quarter of the stir-fry along one side. Scatter with sesame seeds. Roll up firmly.

Makes 4 rolls

1668 kilojoules/400 Calories – per serve
11 g total fat; 3 g saturated fat; 546 mg sodium

Author's note: *East meets Tex Mex, in this recipe which combines the cooking techniques and some ingredients of Asia wrapped up with a tortilla, a traditional bread, from this region of America.*

*Oakleaf, Pear and Walnut
Salad (page 46)*

Stir-fried Tortilla Wrap

*Corn and Wild Rice Fritters
with Tomato*

Oakleaf, Pear and Walnut Salad

2 ripe firm pears, cored

lemon juice

1 red oakleaf lettuce or other red lettuce of your choice
(e.g. coral or mignonette), leaves separated

1/3 cup/35 g unsalted walnut halves, roasted

2 tablespoons crumbled blue cheese

RED WINE PEAR DRESSING

1 canned or blanched fresh pear, with 1 tablespoon
liquid reserved

2 tablespoons red wine or balsamic vinegar

1 teaspoon freshly ground black pepper

1 **Dressing:** Place pear and liquid, vinegar and black pepper in
a blender. Purée.

2 Cut each pear into eight segments. Place in a bowl. Add
lemon juice. Toss to coat – this helps prevent the pears from
browning.

3 Arrange lettuce on a serving platter. Top with pears. Drizzle
with dressing. Scatter with walnuts and cheese.

Serves 4

620 kilojoules/149 Calories – per serve
9 g total fat; 2 g saturated fat; 114 mg sodium

Sushi Hand Rolls

4 sheets nori (roasted seaweed)

wasabi (Japanese horseradish)

SUSHI RICE

2 cups/440 g short or medium grain rice

2 1/4 cups/560 mL water

1 1/2 tablespoons sugar

1/2 teaspoon salt – can be omitted if you prefer

1/2 cup/125 mL rice vinegar

FILLING IDEAS

(All ingredients are cut in long thin strips)

cucumber

carrot

pickled ginger

daikon (white radish)

avocado

sashimi quality raw tuna, salmon, ocean trout or king fish

Hot Tuna Filling (see recipe at right)

FOR SERVING

a mixture of equal quantities of rice wine (mirin) and
reduced-salt soy sauce

wasabi (Japanese horseradish)

pickled ginger

1 **Sushi rice:** Place rice in a large bowl. Pour over cold water
to cover. Swirl vigorously with hands. Drain in a colander.
Repeat washing process 2-3 times until water is clear. Stand
rice in colander for 20-30 minutes.

2 Place rice and the 2 1/4 cups water in a large, heavy-based
saucepan over a high heat. Cover with a tight-fitting lid. Bring to
the boil. Reduce heat to medium. Cook for 5 minutes. Reduce
heat to very low. Steam for 10 minutes longer – don't be
tempted to lift the lid. Remove pan from heat. Stand, covered,
for 10-15 minutes – all the liquid should be absorbed.

3 Meanwhile, place sugar, salt and vinegar in a small non-
reactive saucepan over a medium heat. Heat until sugar dissolves.

4 Turn rice into a large non-metallic bowl. Using a flat wooden
spoon or spatula, fan the rice to cool it while cutting through it in
a slicing, not stirring, motion to separate the grains. At the same
time slowly add the vinegar mixture. Continue until the rice is
warm and there is no steam. Cover with a damp clean cloth
and keep at room temperature – use within the day. Do not
refrigerate or the rice will go hard.

5 To assemble rolls, cut each nori sheet in half. Place one piece,
shiny side down, on a clean dry board. Using wet hands, press
a few tablespoons of the rice down one side leaving a 1-2 cm
border. Spread thinly with a little wasabi – this is very hot and
you may prefer not to use it. Place filling down centre of rice.
Fold one side of nori over the other. Roll up like a cone. Serve
with soy mixture, wasabi and pickled ginger.

Makes 8 hand rolls – allow 2 per serve

878 kilojoules/213 Calories – per roll (made without salt)
less than 1 g total fat; less than 1 g saturated fat; 162 mg sodium

Hot Tuna Hand Rolls: Combine 1/2 cup/125 g diced fresh tuna,
1 tablespoon diced green onions, 1/2 teaspoon sesame oil and
1/4 teaspoon ground chilli. Use as filling for rolls.

oceancatch

Slow-roasted Ocean Trout with Nori Crisps

4 x 150 g ocean trout or salmon fillets, skinned and boned

1 tablespoon reduced-salt soy sauce

2 teaspoons sesame oil

2 sheets nori (roasted seaweed), cut into thin strips

1 bunch/400 g Chinese or English spinach

WASABI YOGURT

3/4 cup/155 g low-fat natural yogurt

1 teaspoon wasabi paste (Japanese horseradish) or to taste

1 teaspoon minced fresh ginger

juice of 1/2 lime or lemon

1   Preheat oven to 75°C. Lightly spray or brush a baking dish with unsaturated oil.

2   Place fish in a single layer in baking dish. Combine soy sauce and sesame oil. Brush over each fillet. Bake for 20-30 minutes or until fish just starts to flake when tested with a fork – the flesh shouldn't change colour, so it won't look cooked, but it melts in your mouth.

3   **Wasabi Yogurt:** Place yogurt, wasabi, ginger and lime juice in a bowl. Mix to combine. Cover. Refrigerate until ready to serve.

4   **Nori crisps:** Heat a nonstick frying pan over a high heat until hot. Add nori strips. Cook, tossing, for 20-30 seconds or until crisp – this happens quickly, so don't leave them. Alternatively, brush nori with a little sesame oil. Sprinkle with sesame seeds and black pepper to taste. Bake at 200°C for about 10 minutes or until crisp – take care if using a fan-forced oven as the fan can blow the nori strips off the baking tray.

5   Steam or blanch spinach until just wilted.

6   To serve, divide spinach between serving plates. Top with fish and nori crisps. Accompany with Wasabi Yogurt and cooked rice or rice noodles.

Serves 4

1450 kilojoules/377 Calories – per serve
8 g total fat; 3 g saturated fat; 335 mg sodium

Calamari and Coriander Spaghetti

500 g calamari (squid), cleaned, tube cut into rings

500 g spaghetti or vermicelli

2 teaspoons olive oil

1 red onion, finely diced

1 clove garlic, crushed

4 plum tomatoes, seeded and diced

1/2 cup/80 g pitted black olives, rinsed and drained, sliced

1/4 cup/60 mL low-salt chicken or fish stock (page 174)

1/4 cup/60 mL dry white wine

1 cup/50 g chopped fresh coriander

3 tablespoons chopped fresh mint

freshly ground black pepper

1   Bring a large saucepan of water to the boil. Using a slotted spoon or wire basket, carefully lower calamari into water. Cook for 5-10 seconds or until it just turns white and is firm. Drain. Plunge into iced water. Drain again. Set aside.

2   Bring a large saucepan of fresh water to the boil. Add pasta. Cook according to packet directions.

3   Meanwhile, place oil, onion and garlic in a nonstick frying pan over a medium heat. Cook, stirring, for 3-4 minutes or until onion is soft. Add tomatoes, olives, stock and wine. Bring to simmering. Simmer for 5 minutes. Stir in coriander, mint, calamari and black pepper to taste. Cook for 1-2 minutes or until heated through.

4   Drain pasta. Add calamari mixture. Toss to combine.

5   To serve, divide pasta mixture between serving bowls. Accompany with crusty Italian bread and a green salad.

Serves 4

2494 kilojoules/599 Calories – per serve
6 g total fat; 1 g saturated fat; 380 mg sodium

Swordfish with Corn and Black Bean Salad

1 teaspoon olive oil

4 x 150 g swordfish steaks

HOT CORN AND BLACK BEAN SALAD

1 teaspoon olive oil

2 large cobs sweet corn, kernels removed

2 green onions, chopped

1/2 red pepper, diced

1 x 315 g cooked or canned black or borlotti beans, rinsed and drained

1/4 cup/75 g diced avocado

3 tablespoons chopped fresh coriander

LIME DRESSING

2 tablespoons lime juice

1 tablespoon raspberry or red wine vinegar

2 teaspoons olive oil

1   **Dressing:** Place lime juice, vinegar and oil in a screwtop jar. Shake to combine. Set aside.

2   **Salad:** Heat oil in a nonstick frying pan or wok over a high heat. Add sweet corn kernels, green onions and red pepper. Stir-fry for 3-4 minutes or until just tender. Add beans, avocado and coriander. Toss to combine. Keep warm.

3   Heat a char-grill pan or barbecue to a high heat. Brush fish with oil. Grill for 2-3 minutes each side or until just tender – the centre should still be moist and slightly undercooked.

4   To serve, divide salad between serving plates. Top with fish. Drizzle with dressing. Serve with crusty bread to scoop up the salad and dressing.

Serves 4

1586 kilojoules/380 Calories – per serve (without bread, using canned beans)
13 g total fat; 3 g saturated fat; 350 mg sodium

Cajun-crusted Fish with Yogurt Sauce

4 x 150 g white fish fillets (e.g. snapper, blue-eye cod, Spanish mackerel or barramundi)

1 tablespoon olive oil

CAJUN SPICE MIX

1 tablespoon paprika

1 teaspoon dried thyme

1 teaspoon freshly ground black pepper

1 teaspoon dry mustard

1/2 teaspoon dried oregano

1/2 teaspoon cayenne pepper

YOGURT SAUCE

1/2 cup/100 g low-fat natural yogurt

1 tablespoon lime or lemon juice

1 small Lebanese cucumber, grated

1 tablespoon chopped fresh dill

1   **Sauce:** Place yogurt, lime juice, cucumber and dill in a bowl. Mix to combine. Cover. Refrigerate until ready to serve.

2   **Spice mix:** Combine paprika, thyme, black pepper, mustard, oregano and cayenne pepper. Brush fish fillets with a little oil. Rub spice mixture onto all surfaces.

3   Heat a char-grill or heavy-based nonstick frying pan over a high heat until very hot. Add remaining oil. Heat until just starting to smoke. Add fish. Cook for 2-3 minutes each side or until surface starts to blacken.

4   Serve on a bed of cooked rice. Accompany with Yogurt Sauce and a fresh salad or steamed vegetables of your choice.

Serves 4

877 kilojoules/209 Calories – per serve
8 g total fat; 2 g saturated fat; 150 mg sodium

Author's note: *Prepared cajun or blackened fish spice mixes are available from specialty herb and spices shops and some delicatessens and supermarkets. They are a useful alternative for when time is short. However, if you are trying to cut down on salt or on a low-salt diet, check the list of ingredients as many of the commercial mixes are high in salt.*
This spice mix can also be used on chicken or pork.

Cajun-crusted Fish with Yogurt Sauce

Swordfish with Corn and Black Bean Salad

Mustard-glazed Tuna on Parsnip Purée

4 x 130 g tuna steaks

2 teaspoons olive oil

MUSTARD GLAZE

2 tablespoons wholegrain or dijon mustard

1 tablespoon honey

1 teaspoon no-added-salt tomato paste

2 tablespoons orange juice

1 tablespoon red wine vinegar or balsamic vinegar

freshly ground black pepper

PARSNIP PUREE

2 parsnips, peeled and chopped

2 potatoes, peeled and chopped

1/4 cup/45 g low-fat natural yogurt or buttermilk

1/2 teaspoon ground white pepper

2 teaspoons horseradish relish, optional

1 **Glaze:** Place mustard, honey, tomato paste, orange juice, vinegar and black pepper to taste in a small saucepan. Bring to the boil. Reduce heat. Simmer until mixture reduces and is of a glaze consistency. Keep hot.

2 **Purée:** Boil or microwave parsnips and potatoes until tender. Drain. Place in a bowl. Add yogurt, white pepper and horseradish relish. Mash, then push through a sieve. Alternatively, place all ingredients in a food processor. Purée. Keep warm or reheat just prior to serving.

3 Heat a char-grill or nonstick frying pan or barbecue until very hot. Brush tuna with oil. Place on cooking surface. Cook for 1-2 minutes. Turn. Spoon glaze over tuna. Cook for 1-2 minutes or until cooked to your liking – the tuna is best if it is moist and still pink in the centre.

4 To serve, place a mound of purée in the centre of each serving plate. Top with tuna. Spoon over glaze. Accompany with steamed green beans or steamed green vegetable of your choice.
Serves 4

1161 kilojoules/277 Calories – per serve
7 g total fat; 1 g saturated fat; 137 mg sodium

Cook's tip: *Swordfish or marlin are good alternatives for this dish.*

Herb-crusted Mahi Mahi with Pawpaw Relish

1 tablespoon extra virgin olive oil

4 x 150 g mahi mahi fillets, skin and bones removed

SESAME HERB CRUST

1 tablespoon sesame seeds

1 tablespoon finely chopped fresh parsley

1 teaspoon dried oregano

1 teaspoon freshly ground black pepper

juice of 2 limes

FRESH PAWPAW RELISH

1/2 cup/95 g diced pawpaw

1/2 red pepper, diced

1 plum tomato, seeded and diced

1 tablespoon chopped fresh coriander

1 tablespoon chopped fresh mint

1 tablespoon lime juice

freshly ground black pepper

1 **Herb crust:** Place sesame seeds, parsley, oregano, black pepper and lime juice in a bowl. Mix to combine.

2 Lightly spray or brush a baking dish with olive oil. Arrange fish in a single layer in dish. Spread herb crust over top of fish, pressing to coat evenly. Cover. Refrigerate for 20 minutes, if time allows.

3 **Relish:** Place pawpaw, red pepper, tomato, coriander, mint, lime juice and black pepper to taste in a bowl. Mix to combine. Cover. Refrigerate until ready to use.

4 Preheat oven to 220°C. Bake fish, uncovered, for 8-10 minutes or until flesh flakes when tested with a fork – cooking time will depend on the thickness of fillets.

5 Serve with relish, steamed rice and a tossed green salad or steamed vegetables of your choice
Serves 4

970 kilojoules/231 Calories – per serve
9 g total fat; 2 g saturated fat; 135 mg sodium

Cook's tip: *Mahi mahi is a mild, firm-textured fish which is becoming quite popular with chefs and home cooks. If it's not available, try this recipe using ocean trout, Spanish mackerel, swordfish, sea bass, blue warehou or blue-eye cod.*

Lemon Myrtle Scented Fish cooked in Paper

1 cup/140 g finely shredded fresh fennel

1/2 red pepper, diced

4 x 150 g firm, mild white fish fillets (e.g. blue-eye cod, ling, jewfish or mahi mahi)

1 green onion, thinly sliced

1 teaspoon ground lemon myrtle

1 tablespoon lime juice

1 tablespoon white wine or rice wine (mirin)

1 tablespoon low-fat natural yogurt

1   Preheat oven to 190°C. Cut four sheets of baking or parchment paper, each about 30 cm long.

2   Place one-quarter of the fennel and red pepper in the centre of each sheet of paper to form a 'bed' for the fish. Place fish on top. Combine green onion, lemon myrtle, lime juice, wine and yogurt. Spread over top of fish. Bring long edges of paper together. Fold over, then twist ends to seal – the fish will steam in its parcel.

3   Place parcels on a baking tray. Bake for 10-15 minutes or until fish flakes when tested with a fork.

4   To serve, place parcels on serving plates. Allow diners to open their own parcel so they can enjoy the escaping aromas – but be sure to warn them about the escaping steam.

Serves 4

1051 kilojoules/286 Calories – per serve
5 g total fat; 2 g saturated fat; 92 mg sodium

Ingredient know-how: *Lemon myrtle is an Australian bush food. It has a deep green leaf that is wonderfully aromatic and reminiscent of lemon grass, lime, lemon and pepper. It can be purchased from specialty food stores and some delicatessens, health food stores and supermarkets. If you can't find it, use a combination of ground lemon grass and ground black pepper or a kaffir lime leaf.*

Citrus and Wine Poached Mackerel

1 red pepper, finely diced

2 green onions, sliced

1-2 cm piece fresh ginger, thinly sliced

1 teaspoon olive oil

1 teaspoon grated orange zest

1/2 cup/125 mL dry white wine

1/3 cup/90 mL orange juice

2 tablespoons lemon juice

1 teaspoon reduced-salt soy sauce

4 x 150 g Spanish mackerel fillets, skin removed

2 tablespoons chopped fresh coriander

freshly ground black pepper

1   Place red pepper, green onions, ginger and oil in a large deep-sided nonstick frying pan with a lid – the pan should be large enough to hold the fish in a single layer. Cook, stirring, over a medium heat for 1-2 minutes or until red pepper is soft. Stir in orange zest, wine, orange and lemon juices and soy sauce. Bring to the boil.

2   Reduce heat. Add fish. Cover. Cook for 5 minutes or until fish just starts to flake when tested with a fork. Using a fish slice or slotted spoon, remove fish from cooking liquid and place on a plate. Cover with aluminium foil. Keep warm in a low oven.

3   Add coriander and black pepper to taste to liquid remaining in pan. Bring to the boil. Boil rapidly until mixture reduces to a sauce consistency.

4   Serve with steamed rice and steamed green vegetables of your choice or a tossed green salad.

Serves 4

875 kilojoules/208 Calories – per serve
4 g total fat; 1 g saturated fat; 144 mg sodium

Cook's tip: *Try this recipe using other fish such as blue-eye cod, bream, sea perch, orange roughy or gemfish.*

Herb-crusted Mahi Mahi with Pawpaw Relish (page 54)

Citrus and Wine Poached Mackerel

Lemon Myrtle Scented Fish cooked in Paper

Prawn, Asparagus and Noodle Stir-fry

100 g thick rice noodles

2 teaspoons peanut or macadamia oil

few drops sesame oil, optional

1 green onion, chopped

1 tablespoon finely chopped fresh ginger

700 g shelled uncooked medium prawns – preferably with tails intact

1 bunch/250 g asparagus, chopped

1/2 cup/15 g lightly packed coriander leaves

ORIENTAL SAUCE

1/4 cup/60 mL low-salt fish or vegetable stock (pages 174 and 175)

2 teaspoons hoisin sauce

1 tablespoon reduced-salt soy sauce

2 tablespoons rice vinegar or white wine

1   Place noodles in a bowl. Pour over boiling water to cover. Soak for 10 minutes – separate noodles with chopsticks or a fork if necessary. Drain. Set aside.

2   **Sauce:** Place stock, hoisin and soy sauces and vinegar in a small bowl. Mix to combine. Set aside.

3   Heat oils in a wok or nonstick frying pan over a medium heat. Add green onion and ginger. Stir-fry 1-2 minutes. Add prawns and asparagus. Stir-fry for 2-3 minutes or until prawns change colour. Add prepared noodles, sauce and coriander. Stir-fry for 2-3 minutes or until heated through. Serve immediately.
Serves 6

1053 kilojoules/249 Calories – per serve
4 g total fat; 1 g saturated fat; 854 mg sodium

Oven-roast Fish Fingers with Tartare

2 cups/180 g oat or corn flakes

3 tablespoons sesame seeds

1 teaspoon dried oregano

1/2 teaspoon dried rosemary

freshly ground black pepper

1 tablespoon chopped fresh parsley and/or chives

1 egg, lightly beaten

2 tablespoons buttermilk or low-fat natural yogurt

1 teaspoon dijon mustard

1/4 cup/45 g wholemeal flour

600 g boneless white fish (e.g. ling, flake or hake, swordfish, gemfish or mahi mahi)

TARTARE SAUCE (OPTIONAL)

2 tablespoons finely chopped gherkin or dill pickles

1/2 cup/100 g low-fat natural yogurt

2 tablespoons no-added-salt tomato paste

1 tablespoon lemon juice

1   Preheat oven to 190°C. Lightly spray or brush a baking tray with unsaturated oil or line with nonstick baking paper.

2   **Tartare Sauce:** Place gherkin, yogurt, tomato paste and lemon juice in a bowl. Mix to combine. Cover. Refrigerate until ready to use.

3   Place oat flakes, sesame seeds, oregano, rosemary and black pepper to taste in a food processor. Process to make fine crumbs. Place in a flat dish. Mix in parsley.

4   Place egg, buttermilk and mustard in a bowl. Whisk to combine.

5   Place flour in a plastic food bag. Add fish. Shake to coat.

6   Shake excess flour from fish. Dip in egg mixture. Roll in crumbs to coat. Dip fish in egg mixture and roll in crumbs a second time. Place on prepared baking tray. Bake for 10-15 minutes or until coating is crisp and golden. Serve with tartare sauce, mashed potatoes and a tossed green salad or steamed green vegetables of your choice.
Serves 4

1991 kilojoules/476 Calories – per serve (with sauce)
11 g total fat; 2 g saturated fat; 251 mg sodium
1848 kilojoules/442 Calories – per serve (without sauce)
11 g total fat; 2 g saturated fat; 161 mg sodium

Fresh Tuna Burgers with Mango Salsa

6 bread rolls of your choice or pieces of focaccia bread, split horizontally

mixed salad greens

FRESH TUNA AND NUT PATTIES

2 teaspoons olive oil

2 green onions, finely chopped

1 tablespoon finely chopped fresh ginger

1 clove garlic, finely chopped

500 g fresh tuna, cut into large pieces

¹/₂ cup/80 g chopped unsalted macadamias, roasted

¹/₂ cup/30 g breadcrumbs, made from stale bread

2 tablespoons chopped fresh coriander

1 egg

freshly ground black pepper

HOISIN AND SOY GLAZE

2 tablespoons hoisin sauce

1 tablespoon reduced-salt soy sauce

1 teaspoon sesame oil

FRESH MANGO SALSA

¹/₂ fresh mango, diced

1 plum tomato, diced

¹/₂ Lebanese cucumber, diced

¹/₂ red onion, diced

2 tablespoons chopped fresh coriander

juice of 1 lime or lemon

1 tablespoon low-fat natural yogurt, optional

1   **Glaze:** Combine hoisin and soy sauces and oil. Set aside.

2   **Salsa:** Place mango, tomato, cucumber, onion, coriander, lime juice and yogurt in a bowl. Mix to combine. Cover. Refrigerate until ready to use.

3   Place oil, green onions, ginger and garlic in a small frying pan over a low heat. Cook, stirring frequently, until soft and fragrant. Remove pan from heat. Cool.

4   Place tuna in a food processor. Process to coarsely mince. Transfer to a bowl. Add nuts, breadcrumbs, coriander, egg, black pepper to taste and spring onion mixture. Mix to combine. Shape into six patties. Place on a plate lined with plastic food wrap. Cover. Refrigerate until ready to cook.

5   Heat a char-grill or heavy-based frying pan over a high heat until hot. Brush patties with glaze. Add to pan. Cook for 3-4 minutes each side – the patties should be moist and slightly pink in the centre.

6   To serve, place salad greens on bottom half of each roll. Top with a pattie, salsa and top of roll. Serve immediately.
Makes 6 burgers

1722 kilojoules/415 Calories – per burger
17 g total fat; 3 g saturated fat; 647 mg sodium

Cook's tip: *These burgers are also delicious made with swordfish, salmon or ocean trout.*

Whole Fish with a Soy Ginger Sauce

4 plate-size or 1-2 large whole fish (e.g. mullet, barramundi, bream, snapper or sea perch), scaled and cleaned

prepared Asian greens of your choice (e.g bok choy, choy sum, Chinese spinach or mizuna)

SOY GINGER SAUCE

3 green onions, thinly sliced

2.5 cm piece fresh ginger, finely chopped

1 clove garlic, finely chopped

1 fresh red chilli, thinly sliced

2 teaspoons sugar

100 mL rice wine (mirin) or sherry

1 tablespoon reduced-salt soy sauce

1 tablespoon fish sauce

juice of 1 lime

1   **Sauce:** Place green onions, ginger, garlic, chilli, sugar, rice wine, soy and fish sauces and lime juice in a small bowl. Mix to combine. Set aside.

2   Preheat grill to a medium heat. Using a sharp knife, make 2-3 deep slashes in each side of fish. Place fish on a grill tray lined with aluminium foil. Cook under grill for 4-5 minutes on each side or until flesh just flakes when tested with a fork – take care not to overcook or the fish will be dry.

3   Meanwhile, place Asian greens in a bamboo steamer. Cover. Steam over simmering water for 3-4 minutes or until cooked. To serve, divide vegetables between plates. Top with fish. Spoon over sauce. Accompany with bowls of steamed rice.
Serves 4

905 kilojoules/216 Calories – per serve
3 g total fat; 1 g saturated fat; 157 mg sodium

Fresh Tuna Burgers with Mango Salsa

Whole Fish with a Soy Ginger Sauce

Salmon Vegetable Parcels

1 small orange sweet potato, cut lengthwise into thin slices

1 large zucchini (courgette), cut lengthwise into thin slices

1 large carrot, cut lengthwise into thin slices

4 large silverbeet or English spinach leaves

4 x 150 g salmon or ocean trout fillets, skinned and boned

1 teaspoon chopped fresh oregano

1 tablespoon chopped fresh parsley

crushed fresh black peppercorns

2-3 sprigs fresh oregano

2-3 large sprigs fresh parsley

water or a mixture of half water and half wine

1   Boil or microwave sweet potato, zucchini and carrot until just tender. Drain well. Set aside. Remove thick white stems from silverbeet. Boil or microwave leaves until they are just starting to wilt. Drain well.

2   Cut four pieces of plastic food wrap, each about 30 cm long. Place on work surface. Place a silverbeet leaf on each piece of food wrap and overlap edges where the stem has been removed. Place a piece of fish in the centre of each leaf. Sprinkle with chopped oregano and parsley and black pepper to taste.

3   Cover fish with sweet potato, zucchini and carrot slices. Wrap silverbeet around fish and vegetables to make parcels. Wrap plastic food wrap around each parcel and tie ends in a knot to seal. Place on a plate. Cover. Refrigerate until ready to cook.

4   Place oregano and parsley sprigs and 5 cm of water in a wok or large saucepan. Bring to simmering. Place fish parcels in a bamboo steamer. Place over wok. Cover. Steam for 10 minutes or until you feel fish just starts to flake when pressed with a fork – the cooked fish should still be pink inside.

5   To serve, remove plastic wrap and accompany with steamed rice or potatoes and steamed vegetables of your choice.

Serves 4

1154 kilojoules/304 Calories – per serve
5 g total fat; 2 g saturated fat; 140 mg sodium

Author's note: *Salmon with the bones removed is available from many fishmongers and supermarkets. If you get stuck and have to do it yourself, the easiest way is to use a pair of flat edged tweezers. I keep an extra pair of tweezers in the kitchen for this purpose. If you'd like to serve a sauce with the parcels try the Cucumber Yogurt Sauce (page 172) or Roasted Chilli Tomato Salsa (page 170).*

outdoorfare

Warm Barbecued Octopus and Potato Salad

500 g baby octopus, cleaned

500 g pink-skinned potatoes (e.g. desiree, pontiac or pink fir), washed

rocket or mixed salad greens

2 Lebanese cucumbers, chopped

2 green onions, finely sliced

LIME AND CHILLI MARINADE

2 tablespoons olive oil

juice of 1 lime or lemon

1 fresh red chilli, diced

1 clove garlic, crushed

TOMATO CONCASSE (OPTIONAL)

4 plum tomatoes, diced

1/2 cup/25 g chopped fresh coriander

1/2 red onion, diced

1/3 cup/90 mL balsamic or sherry vinegar

1 tablespoon olive oil

1 tablespoon lemon juice

freshly ground black pepper

1 **Marinade:** Place oil, lime juice, chilli and garlic in a bowl. Mix to combine. Cut octopus in half lengthwise – if very small, leave whole. Add to marinade. Marinate in the refrigerator overnight – marinating time should be at least 2 hours.

2 Boil or microwave potatoes until tender. Drain. Cool slightly. Cut into bite-sized chunks.

3 **Concasse:** Place tomatoes, coriander, onion, vinegar, oil, lemon juice and black pepper to taste in a bowl. Mix to combine.

4 Preheat barbecue plate or char-grill pan to very hot.

5 Line a serving platter with rocket leaves. Top with potatoes, cucumber and onion. Drain octopus. Cook on barbecue or in pan, turning frequently, for 3–5 minutes or until tentacles curl – take care not to overcook or the octopus will be tough.

6 To serve, spoon hot octopus over prepared salad. Top with concasse, if desired. Accompany with crusty bread.

Serves 6

839 kilojoules/202 Calories – per serve (without concasse)
8 g total fat; 1 g saturated fat; 260 mg sodium
1033 kilojoules/248 Calories – per serve (with concasse)
11 g total fat; 2 g saturated fat; 268 mg sodium

Tropical Chicken Salad

2 large skinless chicken breast fillets

1 Lebanese cucumber, diced

1 cup/190 g diced fresh or unsweetened canned pineapple

1/2 cup/90 g diced pawpaw

1/4 cup/45 g raw unsalted cashews

2 green onions, sliced diagonally

2 tablespoons chopped fresh coriander

2 tablespoons chopped fresh mint

CHILLI AND LIME DRESSING

1 fresh red chilli, thinly sliced

finely grated zest of 1 lime

juice of 2 limes

1 tablespoon fish sauce

1 tablespoon rice wine vinegar

1/2 teaspoon sesame oil

1 Preheat barbecue to a high heat.

2 Cook chicken on barbecue grill for 4–5 minutes each side or until cooked through. Alternatively, place chicken in frying pan, pour over water or a mixture of water and wine to cover. Cover. Bring to simmering. Poach for 10 minutes or until chicken is cooked. Cool. Cut into thin strips.

3 Place chicken, cucumber, pineapple, pawpaw, cashews, green onions, coriander and mint in a bowl. Toss to combine.

4 **Dressing:** Place chilli, lime zest and juice, fish sauce, vinegar and oil in a screwtop jar. Shake to combine. Drizzle dressing over salad. Toss. Cover. Refrigerate for at least 15 minutes before serving – this allows the flavours to develop.

Serves 4

1032 kilojoules/246 Calories – per serve
9 g total fat; 2 g saturated fat; 510 mg sodium

Cook's tip: *If you are in a hurry, buy a cooked chicken to make this salad, but look for stores which do not smother the bird in fat before and during cooking – many stores are now selling cooked skinless chicken.*

Seafood alternative: *This dish is also delicious made using fresh crab or prawns or a mixture of seafood instead of the chicken.*

Grilled Asparagus and Mushroom Bruschetta

1 teaspoon extra virgin olive oil

16 asparagus spears, trimmed

8 large flat mushrooms

4 thick slices crusty Italian bread or ciabatta

4 tablespoons reduced-fat fresh ricotta cheese, optional

crushed black peppercorns

LEMON AND HERB DRESSING

1 tablespoon chopped fresh dill or basil

juice of 1 lemon

2 teaspoons extra virgin olive oil

1 teaspoon balsamic vinegar

1   **Dressing:** Place dill, lemon juice, oil and vinegar in a screwtop jar. Shake well to combine. Set aside.

2   Preheat a barbecue or char-grill pan over a high heat until very hot, then brush with oil.

3   Place asparagus and mushrooms on barbecue or in pan. Cook, turning asparagus several times for 4-5 minutes or until asparagus and mushrooms are tender.

4   When vegetables are almost cooked, place bread on grill. Grill until brown on one side. Turn. Spread with ricotta cheese – if you are not using the ricotta cheese, brush with a little extra virgin olive oil or mild mustard. Cut mushrooms into thick slices. Place mushrooms and asparagus on bread. Drizzle with dressing. Season with black pepper to taste.
Serves 4

885 kilojoules/214 Calories – per serve
7 g total fat; 2 g saturated fat; 300 mg sodium

Sweet Potato and Cannellini Falafel

6 large Lebanese or pita bread rounds

3 tablespoons purchased or homemade hummus (page 177)

2 cups/90 g shredded lettuce

1 cup/180 g purchased or homemade tabbouleh (page 177)

1 red onion, thinly sliced

lemon juice

SWEET POTATO FALAFEL

400 g orange sweet potato, cut into chunks

2 teaspoons olive oil

1 clove garlic, crushed

2 teaspoons ground cumin

1 teaspoon ground coriander

1 tablespoon no-added-salt tomato paste

400 g cooked or canned cannellini beans or chickpeas, rinsed and drained

2 tablespoons chopped fresh coriander

1 tablespoon tahini (sesame seed paste)

1 tablespoon lemon juice

1 cup/60 g breadcrumbs, made from stale bread

1   **Falafel:** Boil or microwave sweet potato until tender. Drain. Place in a bowl. Mash. Set aside.

2   Heat oil in a nonstick frying pan over a medium heat. Add garlic, cumin and ground coriander. Cook, stirring, for 1-2 minutes or until fragrant. Stir in tomato paste. Cook for 3-4 minutes or until it becomes deep red and develops a rich aroma. Stir in beans.

3   Place mixture in a food processor. Add fresh coriander, tahini and lemon juice. Using the pulse button, process to make a coarse paste. Add bean mixture and breadcrumbs to mashed sweet potato. Mix to combine. Shape mixture into small (about 3 cm round) patties. Roll in flour to coat. Place on a plate lined with plastic food wrap. Cover. Refrigerate for at least 30 minutes or until ready to cook – the patties can be made up to this stage a day in advance.

4   Preheat a barbecue or grill to a medium heat. Add falafel. Cook for 3-4 minutes each side or until golden and crispy.

5   Meanwhile, heat bread on barbecue grill. While still hot, spread with hummus. Top with lettuce, tabbouleh and red onion. Place three falafel down one side of each bread round and squash slightly. Sprinkle with lemon juice to taste. Roll up tightly. Serve immediately.
Serves 6

1502 kilojoules/363 Calories – per serve (using canned chickpeas)
7 g total fat; 1 g saturated fat; 542 mg sodium

Grilled Asparagus and Mushroom Bruschetta

Sweet Potato and Cannellini Falafel

Swordfish and Pineapple Kebabs (page 70)

Barbecued Seafood Salad

2 tablespoons lemon juice

1 tablespoon olive oil

300 g firm white fish (e.g. swordfish, mackerel, blue-eye cod or barramundi), cut into 3 cm cubes

300 g pink fish (e.g. salmon, ocean trout, marlin or tuna)

12 scallops

12 uncooked prawns (with or without shell)

1 calamari (squid), cleaned and tube cut into rings, reserve tentacles for another use

1 bunch/250 g watercress, broken into sprigs

1 large red onion, cut into rings

1 telegraph cucumber, sliced thinly

RASPBERRY AND TARRAGON DRESSING

3 tablespoons chopped fresh tarragon

2 tablespoons raspberry or red wine vinegar

2 tablespoons lemon juice

1 tablespoon olive oil

freshly ground black pepper

1   Place lemon juice and oil in a bowl. Whisk to combine. Add white and pink fish, scallops, prawns and calamari. Toss to combine. Cover. Marinate in the refrigerator for 1 hour or until ready to use – do not marinate for longer than 2 hours.

2   **Dressing:** Place tarragon, vinegar, lemon juice, oil and black pepper to taste in a screwtop jar. Shake to combine. Set aside.

3   Preheat a barbecue or char-grill pan until very hot. Line a serving platter with watercress.

4   Drain seafood mixture. Place on barbecue plate or in pan. Add onion. Cook, turning several times, for 6-8 minutes or until seafood is just cooked – take care not to overcook or the seafood will be tough and dry.

5   Transfer seafood mixture to a bowl. Add cucumber and dressing. Toss to combine. Spoon seafood mixture over watercress. Serve immediately.

Serves 8

809 kilojoules/193 Calories – per serve
7 g total fat; 1 g saturated fat; 282 mg sodium

Cook's tip: *When making this salad, the prawns can be left whole with the shells on, if you wish. The presentation will be more attractive but eating will be a little messier.*

Swordfish and Pineapple Kebabs

700 g swordfish steaks, cut into large cubes

1/2 fresh pineapple, cut into cubes the same size as the fish

1 green pepper, cut into pieces the same size as the fish

FRESH MINT MARINADE

3 tablespoons chopped fresh mint

2 teaspoons mint relish

1/4 cup/60 mL white wine

juice of 1/2 lime or lemon

2 tablespoons red wine vinegar

1 teaspoon olive oil

freshly ground black pepper

1   Soak 12 bamboo skewers in water for 10 minutes – this prevents them burning during cooking. Thread swordfish, pineapple and green pepper, alternately onto the skewers. Place prepared skewers in a shallow glass or ceramic dish.

2   **Marinade:** Place mint, mint relish, wine, lime juice, vinegar, oil and black pepper to taste in a screwtop jar. Shake to combine. Pour over skewers. Cover. Marinate in the refrigerator for 15 minutes.

3   Preheat barbecue or grill until hot. Lightly spray or brush with unsaturated oil. Cook kebabs on barbecue or under grill for 3-5 minutes each side or until fish just starts to flake when tested with a fork.

Makes 12 kebabs

365 kilojoules/87 Calories – per kebab
1 g total fat; less than 1 g saturated fat; 59 mg sodium

Orange and Almond Couscous Salad

1 cup/250 mL apple juice

1 cup/185 g couscous

1/2 red pepper, diced

4 tablespoons chopped fresh parsley

3 tablespoons chopped fresh mint

1/4 cup/35 g currants

2 oranges, peeled, halved and thinly sliced

1 small red onion, sliced

1/3 cup/30 g slivered unsalted almonds, toasted

WARM CITRUS DRESSING

juice of 1 orange

juice of 1 lemon or lime

2 teaspoons olive or hazelnut oil

1 teaspoon honey

1   Place apple juice in a saucepan over a medium heat. Bring to the boil. Slowly stir in couscous. Remove pan from heat. Cover. Cool. Fluff up with a fork.

2   Add red pepper, parsley, mint and currants to couscous. Toss to combine. Transfer to a serving bowl. Scatter with orange slices and onion.

3   **Dressing:** Place orange and lemon juices, oil and honey in a small saucepan. Place over a low heat to dissolve honey – do not allow mixture to boil. Drizzle dressing over salad. Scatter with almonds.
Serves 6

957 kilojoules/232 Calories – per serve
5 g total fat; less than 1 g saturated fat; 15 mg sodium

Oriental Coleslaw

1 daikon (white radish)

1 large carrot

1/2 Chinese cabbage, shredded

1/4 red cabbage, shredded

2 green onions, cut into long thin strips

18 snow peas (mangetout), cut lengthwise into thin strips

1 cup/40 g shredded spinach

1/2 cup/60 g raisins

1/2 cup/80 g slivered unsalted almonds, toasted, optional

ORIENTAL DRESSING

2 tablespoons sesame seeds

3 teaspoons grated fresh ginger or shredded pickled ginger

1 teaspoon sugar

3 tablespoons rice wine (mirin) or sherry

2 tablespoons rice or wine vinegar

2 teaspoons macadamia or peanut oil

2 teaspoons reduced-salt soy sauce

few drops sesame oil, optional

1   Using a zester, Japanese grater or sharp knife, cut daikon and carrot into long thin strips. Place in a large bowl. Add Chinese and red cabbages, green onions, snow peas, spinach, raisins and nuts. Toss to combine.

2   **Dressing:** Place sesame seeds in a small saucepan over a medium heat. Cook, shaking pan frequently, for 2-3 minutes or until seeds are toasted. Stir in ginger, sugar, mirin, vinegar, macadamia oil, soy sauce and sesame oil. Remove pan from heat. Immediately pour over salad. Toss to combine.
Serves 6

741 kilojoules/178 Calories – per serve
12 g total fat; 1 g saturated fat; 83 mg sodium

Oriental Coleslaw

*Open Marinated Minute Steak
Sandwich (page 74)*

*Orange and Almond
Couscous Salad*

Herb-crusted Barbecued Lamb Salad

700 g lamb eye of loin, in one piece, trimmed of visible fat

olive oil

3 cups/150 g baby English spinach leaves

1/4 cup/50 g kalamata olives, rinsed and drained

250 g cherry tomatoes, halved

250 g green beans or fresh asparagus spears, lightly blanched

ROSEMARY AND LEMON PASTE

2 tablespoons fresh rosemary leaves or 1 tablespoon dried rosemary

1 teaspoon fresh oregano

1 teaspoon crushed black peppercorns

1 teaspoon finely grated lemon zest

1 tablespoon lemon juice

ORANGE DRESSING

1 shallot, finely chopped

1 teaspoon brown sugar

1/4 cup/60 mL sherry vinegar

1/4 cup/60 mL orange juice

2 teaspoons extra virgin olive oil

freshly ground black pepper

1 **Paste:** Place rosemary, oregano, black pepper and lemon zest and juice in a mortar. Pound to make a paste. Place lamb in a shallow glass or ceramic dish. Lightly brush with oil. Spread with paste. Cover. Marinate in the refrigerator for at least 2 hours or overnight.

2 **Dressing:** Place shallot, brown sugar, vinegar, orange juice, oil and black pepper to taste in a screwtop jar. Shake to combine. Set aside.

3 Preheat a barbecue or char-grill pan to a high heat.

4 Place lamb on barbecue or in pan. Cook for 5 minutes each side or until cooked to your liking. Remove lamb from heat. Cover with aluminium foil. Rest for 10 minutes. Cut into thin slices. Place in a bowl. Add half the dressing. Toss to combine.

5 Place spinach, olives, tomatoes and asparagus in a bowl. Add remaining dressing. Toss to combine. Transfer to serving platter. Arrange lamb slices on top.

Serves 6

815 kilojoules/193 Calories – per serve
7 g total fat; 2 g saturated fat; 104 mg sodium

Open Marinated Minute Steak Sandwich

4 x 125 g minute steaks, trimmed of visible fat

4 thick slices sourdough or rye bread

mustard or chutney

3 tomatoes, sliced

1 telegraph cucumber, thinly sliced

crushed black peppercorns

SPICY GINGER MARINADE

2 tablespoons mango chutney

2 green onions, thinly sliced

2 teaspoons minced fresh ginger

2 teaspoons sesame seeds, toasted

2 tablespoons sherry, bourbon or apple juice

1 tablespoon reduced-salt soy sauce

1 tablespoon cider or rice vinegar

1 **Marinade:** Place chutney, green onions, ginger, sesame seeds, sherry, soy sauce and vinegar in a bowl. Whisk to combine.

2 Place steaks in a single layer in a shallow glass or ceramic dish. Pour over marinade. Cover. Marinate in the refrigerator for at least 15 minutes.

3 Preheat a barbecue or grill to a high heat. Drain steaks. Cook on barbecue or under grill, brushing occasionally with marinade, for 5-8 minutes each side or until cooked to your liking.

4 When the steaks are almost cooked, add bread and grill until golden. Spread one side of each slice of bread with mustard. Top with tomato, steak and cucumber. Season with black pepper to taste. Serve with a tossed green salad.

Serves 4

1865 kilojoules/445 Calories – per serve
11 g total fat; 4 g saturated fat; 687 mg sodium

Herb-crusted Barbecued Lamb Salad

Mediterranean Pork and Apple Burgers (page 76)

Thai Prawn Cakes

500 g uncooked peeled prawns, deveined

1/4 cup/30 g chopped green onions

1 teaspoon ground lemon grass

2 kaffir lime or lemon myrtle leaves, soaked in boiling water for 15 minutes, finely chopped, optional

1 egg white

1 tablespoon fish sauce

1 tablespoon fresh lime juice

1 teaspoon sweet chilli sauce or to taste

1/4 cup/15 g breadcrumbs, made from stale bread

2 tablespoons chopped fresh mint

2 tablespoons chopped fresh coriander

CORIANDER DIPPING SAUCE

2 tablespoons chopped fresh coriander

1 green onion, finely chopped

1 clove garlic, crushed

1 teaspoon brown or palm sugar

1/4 cup/60 mL rice or sherry vinegar

2 teaspoons reduced-salt soy sauce

1/2 teaspoon chilli sauce, optional

1   Place prawns in a food processor. Using the pulse button, process to roughly chop. Add green onions, ground lemon grass, lime leaves, egg white, fish sauce, lime juice and chilli sauce. Using the pulse button, process until just combined. Transfer mixture to a bowl. Fold in breadcrumbs, mint and coriander.

2   Shape mixture into 4 cm round patties. Place on a plate lined with plastic food wrap or thread 2-3 patties on a lemon grass skewer (see Cook's tip below). Cover. Refrigerate for 30 minutes or until patties are firm.

3   Preheat a barbecue to a medium heat. Add patties. Cook for 2-3 minutes each side or until lightly browned. Alternatively, heat a nonstick frying pan over a medium heat. Lightly spray or brush with unsaturated oil and pan-fry, or cook under a medium grill or bake in the oven at 210°C – if baking do not thread onto lemon grass skewers.

4   **Sauce:** Place coriander, green onion, garlic, sugar, vinegar and fish, soy and chilli sauces in a bowl. Whisk to combine. Serve with prawn cakes for dipping.

Serves 4 as a main meal or 8 as a starter

627 kilojoules/148 Calories – per serve (as a main meal)
1 g total fat; less than 1 g saturated fat; 1022 mg sodium
313 kilojoules/74 Calories – per serve (as a starter)
less than 1 g total fat; less than 1 g saturated fat; 511 mg sodium

Cook's tip: *Crab or white fish fillets can be used instead of prawns to make these fish cakes. For an attractive presentation and added flavour, thread prepared prawn cakes onto fresh lemon grass stems, then cook on the barbecue. Soak the lemon grass stems in cold water for 1 hour before using – this helps prevent the skewers from burning during cooking.*

Mediterranean Pork and Apple Burgers

2 small granny smith or gala apples, peeled, cored and cut into 6 thick rings

6 thick slices mozzarella cheese, cut to the same size as the apple rings

6 rolls, split and toasted

lettuce leaves of your choice

PORK PATTIES

750 g lean pork mince

1 small red onion, diced

2-3 tablespoons chopped fresh herbs (e.g. coriander, parsley or chives)

1 teaspoon dried sage

1 egg, beaten

dash tabasco or chilli sauce, optional

freshly ground black pepper

1   Preheat barbecue or char-grill pan to a medium heat.

2   **Patties:** Place mince, onion, fresh herbs, sage, egg and tabasco and black pepper to taste in a bowl. Mix to combine. Using wet hands, shape mixture into six patties – make patties 1 cm larger than the apple rings.

3   Lightly spray or brush barbecue grill or pan with unsaturated oil. Add burgers. Cook for 5 minutes. Turn over. Top each pattie with a slice of cheese. Cook for 5-7 minutes or until patties are cooked through and cheese starts to melt. At the same time, cook apple slices for 1-2 minutes each side or until golden. To serve, cover base of each roll with lettuce leaves. Top with patties and apple slices. Accompany with a green salad.

Makes 6 burgers

1520 kilojoules/364 Calories – per burger
9 g total fat; 4 g saturated fat; 531 mg sodium

orientalinfluence

Warm Thai Beef and Mushroom Salad (page 80)

Warm Thai Beef and Mushroom Salad

250 g shiitake mushrooms, stems removed and cut into quarters

250 g oyster mushrooms, stems removed and cut into quarters

1/2 cup/125 mL rice wine (mirin) or dry white wine

1 small fresh red chilli, minced

2 teaspoons freshly ground black pepper

1 teaspoon grated lime zest

500 g lean beef steak (e.g. fillet, topside or round), trimmed of visible fat

1 teaspoon sugar

1/4 cup/60 mL low-salt chicken or vegetable stock (pages 174 and 175)

juice of 1 lime

2 tablespoons fish sauce

2 green onions or shallots, thinly sliced

1 cup/30 g fresh Thai or sweet basil leaves

1/2 cup/10 g fresh mint leaves

2 tablespoons chopped fresh coriander

2 tablespoons chopped dry roasted unsalted cashews or peanuts

1   Preheat grill to a very high heat.

2   Place mushrooms and wine in a non-reactive saucepan over a medium heat. Bring to the boil. Cook, stirring occasionally, for 2-3 minutes or until mushrooms are tender. Using a slotted spoon, remove mushrooms from wine. Drain well. Set aside. Reserve cooking liquid.

3   Place chilli, black pepper and lime zest in a mortar. Using pestle, grind to make a coarse paste. Rub paste over beef. Cook under grill for 1-2 minutes on each side, or until just browned – the beef should be very rare. Remove beef from grill. Rest for 5 minutes. Cut, across the grain, into very thin slices. Set aside.

4   Stir sugar, stock, lime juice and fish sauce into reserved cooking liquid. Place over a medium heat. Bring to the boil. Remove from heat.

5   Add meat. Turn to coat. Transfer meat mixture to a bowl. Add green onions, basil, mint and reserved mushrooms. Toss to combine.

6   To serve, pile salad onto a serving platter. Scatter with coriander and peanuts. Accompany with steamed jasmine rice.
Serves 6-8

541 kilojoules/128 Calories – per serve
3 g total fat; 1 g saturated fat; 556 mg sodium

Cook's tip: *If you wish, other mushrooms of your choice can be used in place of the shiitake and oyster mushrooms.*

Pad Thai with Chicken and Prawns

250 g packet Thai rice stick noodles or wide rice noodles

2 teaspoons unsaturated oil

2 cloves garlic, crushed

2 skinless chicken breast fillets, trimmed of visible fat, cut into 1-2 cm cubes

100 g uncooked medium prawns, deveined, optional

1 red pepper, chopped

2 tablespoons fish sauce

1/4 cup/60 mL lime juice

2 tablespoons low-salt chicken stock (page 174) or white wine

1 egg or 2 egg whites, beaten

2 cups/180 g bean sprouts

1/2 cup/25 g chopped fresh coriander

2 green onions, finely chopped

2 tablespoons chopped dry roasted unsalted macadamias or cashews

1   Place noodles in a bowl. Pour over boiling water to cover. Soak for 15-20 minutes – separate noodles with chopsticks or a fork if necessary. Drain. Set aside.

2   Heat oil in a wok or nonstick frying pan over a medium heat. Add garlic. Stir-fry for 1 minute. Increase heat to high. Add chicken. Stir-fry for 2 minutes or until just cooked. Add prawns and red pepper. Stir-fry for 1 minute or until prawns just change colour.

3   Stir in fish sauce, lime juice and stock. Stir-fry for 1 minute.

4   Pour in egg. Cook, without stirring, until egg just sets.

5   Add bean sprouts and prepared noodles. Cook, tossing, for 3 minutes or until heated through. Scatter with coriander, green onions and cashews. Serve immediately.
Serves 4

1229 kilojoules/294 Calories – per serve
9 g total fat; 1 g saturated fat; 937 mg sodium

Pad Thai with Chicken and Prawns

Grilled Sesame Chicken with Ginger Rice

500 g skinless chicken breast or thigh fillets, or tenderloin, trimmed of visible fat

SOY AND HONEY MARINADE

1 tablespoon sesame seeds, toasted

1 tablespoon rice wine (mirin) or sherry

2 teaspoons honey or plum sauce

2 teaspoons reduced-salt soy sauce

2 teaspoons oyster sauce

1 teaspoon sesame oil

GINGER RICE

1 tablespoon finely chopped fresh ginger

1 teaspoon sesame oil

1 cup/220 g short or medium grain rice, rinsed and drained

330 mL ginger beer

1 tablespoon diced pickled or preserved ginger

1 tablespoon finely chopped green onion, optional

1   **Marinade:** Place sesame seeds, wine, honey, soy and oyster sauces and sesame oil in a non-reactive bowl. Mix to combine.

2   Cut chicken into large pieces. Add to marinade. Toss to coat. Cover. Marinate in the refrigerator for at least 1 hour.

3   **Rice:** Place fresh ginger and sesame oil in a large saucepan over a low heat. Cook, stirring occasionally, for 5 minutes. Add rice. Cook, stirring, for 2 minutes. Stir in ginger beer and pickled ginger. Bring to the boil. Reduce heat. Cover. Steam for 10-15 minutes or until liquid is absorbed and rice is cooked. Stir in green onion.

4   Meanwhile, preheat grill or barbecue to a medium heat. Drain chicken. Cook under grill or on barbecue, brushing occasionally with marinade, for 6-7 minutes or until cooked through and slightly crispy on the outside. The chicken is cooked when the juices run clear when pressed with a fork. Serve chicken with Ginger Rice and steamed Chinese greens.
Serves 4

1773 kilojoules/427 Calories – per serve
7 g total fat; 1 g saturated fat; 264 mg sodium

Caramelised Pork Loin with Lettuce

2 x 200-250 g pork loin fillets, trimmed of visible fat

2 green onions, cut into 5 cm batons

1 red pepper, cut into thin strips

1 butter, mignonette or cos lettuce, leaves separated

MARINADE

1 tablespoon brown sugar

2 teaspoons grated fresh ginger

1 teaspoon Chinese five spice powder

1 tablespoon reduced-salt soy sauce

1 tablespoon rice wine (mirin) or sherry

1 tablespoon oyster sauce

1 teaspoon sesame oil

1 cinnamon stick

SESAME AND HERB DRESSING

1 tablespoon shredded fresh basil

1 tablespoon chopped fresh coriander

2 tablespoons rice or white wine vinegar

1 teaspoon reduced-salt soy sauce

1/2 teaspoon sesame oil

1   **Marinade:** Place sugar, ginger, five spice powder, soy sauce, wine, oyster sauce and sesame oil in a bowl. Mix to combine. Add cinnamon stick.

2   Place pork in a shallow glass or ceramic dish. Pour over marinade. Turn pork to coat. Cover. Marinate in the refrigerator, turning occasionally, for at least 2 hours or overnight.

3   Preheat oven to 220°C.

4   Drain pork. Reserve marinade. Place pork in a baking dish. Bake, uncovered, brushing occasionally with reserved marinade, for 25-30 minutes or until cooked to your liking. Cover loosely with aluminium foil. Rest for 10 minutes. Place green onions and red pepper in a separate baking dish. Bake for 5 minutes or until vegetables soften slightly.

5   **Dressing:** Place basil, coriander, vinegar, soy sauce and oil in a screwtop jar. Shake well to combine.

6   To serve, line a serving platter with lettuce leaves. Cut pork into thick slices. Arrange green onions, red pepper and pork on top of lettuce. Drizzle with dressing. Accompany with steamed rice or udon noodles.
Serves 4

916 kilojoules/219 Calories – per serve
7 g total fat; 1 g saturated fat; 489 mg sodium

Grilled Sesame Chicken with Ginger Rice

Caramelised Pork Loin with Lettuce

Tandoori Lamb

4 x 150-170 g lamb fillets, or 1 rack of lamb, containing 8 cutlets – allow 2 cutlets per serve, trimmed of visible fat

1 quantity Tandoori Marinade (recipe below)

2-3 sprigs fresh rosemary

1 Place lamb in a glass or ceramic dish. Spoon over marinade. Rub in well. Cover. Marinate in the refrigerator for 2-4 hours.

2 Preheat oven to 250°C.

3 Scrape excess marinade from lamb. Place lamb on a wire rack set in a roasting dish. Pour 2-3 cm water or wine into the dish – this helps keep the meat moist during cooking and the dish is easier to clean. Add rosemary sprigs to water.

4 Cook lamb for 12-15 minutes. Turn. Cook for 5-10 minutes longer or until cooked to your liking.

5 Serve with Cucumber Yogurt Sauce (page 172), naan bread, steamed basmati rice and a green salad.

Serves 4

893 kilojoules/209 Calories – per serve
6 g total fat; 3 g saturated fat; 151 mg sodium

Tandoori Fish

4 x 150 g firm white fish fillets (e.g. blue-eye cod, sea bass, warehou, swordfish or mahi mahi)

1 quantity Tandoori Marinade (recipe follows)

1 Place fish in a shallow glass or ceramic dish. Spoon over marinade. Turn fish to coat. Cover. Marinate in the refrigerator for 2-4 hours.

2 Heat a grill or char-grill pan to a high heat. Scrape excess marinade from fish. Place on cooking surface. Cook for 3 minutes each side or until fish flakes when tested with a fork.

3 Serve with Cucumber Yogurt Sauce (page 172), naan bread, steamed basmati rice and a green salad.

Serves 4

689 kilojoules/161 Calories – per serve
2 g total fat; 1 g saturated fat; 154 mg sodium

Tandoori Marinade

1 tablespoon grated fresh ginger

2 teaspoons coriander seeds, toasted

2 teaspoons fresh rosemary leaves

1 teaspoon grated lemon zest

1/2 teaspoon ground cardamom

1/2 teaspoon ground cumin

1/4 teaspoon crushed black peppercorns

1/4 teaspoon chilli sauce or powder

1/2 cup/100 g low-fat natural yogurt

1 tablespoon lemon juice

Place ginger, coriander seeds, rosemary, lemon zest, cardamom, cumin, black peppercorns, chilli sauce, yogurt and lemon juice in a bowl. Mix to combine. Use as desired, see recipes above.

327 kilojoules/66 Calories – analysis for total quantity
less than 1 g total fat; less than 1 g saturated fat; 105 mg sodium

Cook's tip: *For a zap of colour, add 1 tablespoon paprika to the marinade. The tandoori marinade and method of cooking can also be used for whole fish and chicken breast fillets – just adjust the cooking times as necessary.*

Malaysian Grilled Chicken

4 skinless chicken breasts on the bone

2 teaspoons cornflour blended with 2 tablespoons water

cucumber slices

red pepper strips, optional

SPICY ORIENTAL MARINADE

1 red onion, quartered

2 cloves garlic, chopped

1 tablespoon grated fresh ginger

1 tablespoon ground coriander

1 tablespoon palm sugar, crumbled, or brown sugar

1 teaspoon Chinese five spice powder

1/4 cup/60 mL rice wine (mirin)

1/4 cup/60 mL orange or lime juice

1 tablespoon reduced-salt thick dark soy sauce

1   **Marinade:** Place onion and garlic in a food processor. Process to finely chop. Transfer to a bowl. Add ginger, coriander, sugar, five spice powder, wine, orange juice and soy sauce. Mix to combine.

2   Place chicken in a shallow glass or ceramic dish. Pour over marinade. Turn to coat. Cover. Marinate in the refrigerator overnight. Transfer chicken and marinade to a large nonstick frying pan.

3   Place pan over a medium heat. Bring to the boil. Reduce heat. Simmer for 15-20 minutes or until chicken is just tender – take care not to overcook. Using a slotted spoon, remove chicken from cooking liquid. Place in a clean dish. Cover. Refrigerate until ready to barbecue or stir-fry. Reserve marinade.

4   Preheat barbecue to a medium heat. Cook chicken on barbecue grill for 5 minutes each side or until richly coloured and heated through. Alternatively, heat a little oil in a wok over a high heat. Add chicken. Stir-fry for 3-4 minutes or until heated through.

5   Place reserved marinade and cornflour mixture in a small saucepan over a medium heat. Cook, stirring constantly, for 4-5 minutes or until sauce boils and thickens.

6   To serve, spoon sauce over chicken and accompany with cucumber, red pepper and steamed rice.

Serves 4

1236 kilojoules/294 Calories – per serve
5 g total fat; 1 g saturated fat; 317 mg sodium

Author's note: *An icon of Asian cooking in Australia would have to be Carol Selvarajah who inspired me with this cooking style. In her original recipe, tamarind was used, so you could use it instead of the citrus juice if you prefer.*

Singapore Sling (page 88)
Malaysian Grilled Chicken

Gado Gado

PEANUT SAUCE

1 teaspoon unsaturated oil

2 cloves garlic, crushed

1-2 fresh red chillies, according to taste, minced

1/2 cup/125 g no-added-salt crunchy peanut butter

2 teaspoons sugar

2 teaspoons reduced-salt soy sauce

1 teaspoon lemon juice

1 cup/250 mL evaporated skim milk

3/4 cup/185 mL water or low-salt stock (page 174)

VEGETABLES SELECTION – A GUIDE ONLY

1 cup/180 g sliced blanched spinach

10 steamed green beans

1/2 cup/80 g cooked cabbage, cut in squares

1 cup/90 g mung bean sprouts

1 long large potato, cooked and cut into rounds

1 cucumber, peeled and cut into chunks

2 green onions, lightly blanched and cut into batons

1 carrot, cut into batons

1 red banana pepper, cut into strips

1 **Sauce:** Heat oil in a nonstick saucepan or high-sided frying pan. Add garlic and chilli. Cook, stirring, for 1 minute. Stir in peanut butter, sugar, soy sauce and lemon juice. Cook, stirring for 5 minutes. Add evaporated milk and 1/2 cup/125 mL of the water. Cook, stirring constantly, for 4-5 minutes or until sauce thickens. If it becomes too thick, add a little more water. Pour sauce into a serving bowl.

2 To serve, place bowl in the centre of a large serving platter. Arrange vegetables attractively around it.

Serves 6

868 kilojoules/210 Calories – per serve (analysis will vary depending on vegetables used)
12 g total fat; 2 g saturated fat; 174 mg sodium

Author's note: *An Indonesian dish, Gado Gado is perfect for the communal Indonesian-style of eating. Friends will be delighted if you bring this to a 'take a plate' gathering. It's colourful (limited only by the range of vegetables you choose) and the delicious spicy peanut sauce makes a plate of vegetables an exotic experience. Traditionally, the sauce uses coconut milk, but as it is high in saturated fat, I have substituted evaporated skim milk. It still complements the flavours and texture, but, if you want that coconut flavour, add a few drops of coconut essence or see page 187 for a coconut milk substitute. My thanks to Chris Woen of Borobudur Restaurant for his tips and ideas for adapting this recipe.*

Ingredient know-how: *Many people think peanut butter is an unhealthy treat. In fact, the oil in peanuts is mostly mono-unsaturated – one of the kinds that is preferable for lowering blood cholesterol. So, even though peanut butter (and peanuts) are relatively high in fat and calories (less though than butter and margarine), it is a great substitute for spreading on sandwiches and using to thicken sauces – yummy too!*

Singapore Sling

400 g dried thin rice sticks (e.g. Singapore or maifun noodles)

1 tablespoon unsaturated oil

1 tablespoon grated fresh ginger

1 clove garlic, crushed

1 teaspoon curry powder

1 large carrot, thinly sliced diagonally – you should have about 1 1/2 cups of sliced carrots

250 g pork fillet, trimmed of visible fat, thinly sliced

1 cup/90 g bean sprouts

1/2 teaspoon ground cinnamon, optional

1/4 cup/60 mL low-salt stock (page 174) or water

2 tablespoons reduced-salt soy sauce

2 green onions, thinly sliced

1 Place noodles in a bowl. Pour over boiling water to cover. Soak for 20 minutes or until soft. Drain. Rinse under cold water. Drain again. Set aside.

2 Heat oil in a wok or nonstick frying pan over a medium heat. Add ginger and garlic. Stir-fry for 1 minute. Add curry powder and carrots. Stir-fry for 1 minute.

3 Add pork. Stir-fry for 1-2 minutes or until lightly browned. Add bean sprouts, cinnamon, stock, soy sauce and noodles. Stir-fry for 5 minutes or until heated through.

4 To serve, divide between warm bowls. Scatter with green onions.

Serves 6

644 kilojoules/155 Calories – per serve
4 g total fat; less than 1 g saturated fat; 293 mg sodium

Scallop and Mango Sangchssajang

600 g scallops

1 tablespoon cornflour

2 teaspoons brown sugar

2 teaspoons olive or peanut (groundnut) oil

2 shallots, thinly sliced

1 tablespoon grated fresh ginger

6 spears fresh asparagus, chopped

1/2 cup/125 mL rice wine (mirin) or dry white wine

2 tablespoons lime or lemon juice

2 teaspoons fish sauce, optional

2 teaspoons reduced-salt soy sauce

few drops chilli sauce or 1 small fresh red chilli, thinly sliced

1 mango, flesh diced

2 tablespoons shredded fresh sweet basil or coriander

2 cups/370 g hot cooked jasmine or calrose rice

1 butter lettuce or radicchio, leaves separated

1   Place scallops, cornflour and sugar in a plastic food bag. Toss gently to coat.

2   Heat 1 teaspoon of the oil in a nonstick frying pan over a high heat. Add scallops. Stir-fry for 2-3 minutes or until scallops are just cooked. Remove scallops from pan. Set aside.

3   Add remaining oil to pan. Heat. Add shallots and ginger. Stir-fry for 1 minute or until soft. Add asparagus, wine, lime juice and fish, soy and chilli sauces. Stir-fry for 4 minutes or until the asparagus is tender. Add mango and basil. Toss to combine.

4   To serve, spoon rice into lettuce cups, then spoon in some of the scallop mixture. To eat, fold lettuce around scallops and eat in your hands.

Serves 4 as a light meal or 6 as a starter

1238 kilojoules/298 Calories – per serve (as a light meal)
4 g total fat; 1 g saturated fat; 585 mg sodium
825 kilojoules/198 Calories – per serve (as a starter)
3 g total fat; less than 1 g saturated fat; 390 mg sodium

Author's note: *If desired, serve with the dipping sauce used in the recipe for Oyster Spring Rolls (page 26).*

Teppanyaki Sesame Tofu with Soba

1 teaspoon sesame oil

2 tablespoons teriyaki sauce

400 g firm tofu, cut into 4 thick slices

2 tablespoons sesame seeds

1 tablespoon rice wine (mirin)

2 teaspoons reduced-salt soy sauce

1 tablespoon peanut (groundnut) oil

1 carrot, cut into thin strips

16 snow peas (mangetout) or snake (yard long) beans

1 cup/90 g bean sprouts

2 green onions, white parts cut into 5 cm batons and green tops shredded for garnish

2 cups/60 g watercress, broken into sprigs

250 g soba noodles or rice noodles, prepared according to packet directions

1   Heat a large flat frying or char-grill pan to very hot.

2   While pan is heating, place sesame oil and 1 tablespoon of the teriyaki sauce in a small bowl. Mix to combine. Brush over both sides of tofu. Sprinkle one side of each piece of tofu with half the sesame seeds. Combine remaining teriyaki sauce, rice wine and soy sauce. Set aside.

3   Brush pan with a little of the peanut oil. Add tofu, seed side down. Cook for 2 minutes. Sprinkle remaining sesame seeds over tofu. Turn over. Cook for 2 minutes longer or until crisp. Remove tofu from pan. Keep warm.

4   Brush pan with a little more oil. Add carrot, snow peas, bean sprouts and green onion batons. Stir-fry for 2-3 minutes or until tender crisp.

5   Add reserved soy sauce mixture. Stir-fry for 1 minute longer.

6   To serve, divide hot noodles between serving bowls. Top with watercress. Spoon over vegetables and top with tofu. Garnish with shredded green onion tops. Serve with a Japanese-style salad, if desired.

Serves 4

1494 kilojoules/360 Calories – per serve
13 g total fat; 4 g saturated fat; 833 mg sodium

Scallop and Mango Sangchssajang

Teppanyaki Sesame Tofu with Soba

Crab and Pickled Cucumber Salad

400 g fresh crab meat or canned crab meat, rinsed and drained

1 tablespoon lime juice

freshly ground black pepper, optional

toasted sesame seeds, optional

chilli flakes, optional

PICKLED CUCUMBER SALAD

3 cucumbers, cut in half lengthwise

1 tablespoon salt – for curing cucumber

1 small daikon (white radish), peeled and cut into thin strips

3 green onions, chopped

1 tablespoon finely chopped fresh ginger

1 tablespoon sugar

1/4 teaspoon sweet chilli sauce

FRESH CORIANDER DRESSING

3 tablespoons chopped fresh coriander

3 tablespoons white wine or rice wine vinegar

2 teaspoons unsaturated oil

1   **Salad:** Place cucumbers, skin side down, on a plate. Sprinkle with salt. Cover. Stand at room temperature for 1-2 hours.

2   Place daikon, green onions, ginger, sugar and chilli sauce in a bowl. Pour over 1/4 cup/60 mL boiling water. Mix to combine. Cool.

3   Scrape salt from cucumbers. Place cucumbers in a shallow dish. Pour over boiling water to cover. Remove cucumbers immediately. Rinse well under cold water. Pat dry with absorbent kitchen paper. Using a sharp knife, cut cucumbers into thin slices. Place in a bowl.

4   Drain radish mixture. Rinse well under cold water. Drain again. Add to cucumber mixture. Add crab and lime juice.

5   **Dressing:** Place coriander, vinegar and oil in a small bowl. Mix to combine. Pour over salad. Toss to combine.

6   If desired, serve scattered with black pepper or sesame seeds and/or chilli flakes.
Serves 6

319 kilojoules/76 Calories – per serve
2 g total fat; less than 1 g saturated fat; 279 mg sodium

Baked Lime and Lemon Grass Fish

2 green onions, thinly sliced diagonally

2 tablespoons chopped fresh coriander

2 teaspoons grated fresh ginger

1 teaspoon ground lemon grass or 1 teaspoon bottled sliced lemon grass

1 fresh red Thai or bird's eye chilli, finely chopped

2 tablespoons lime juice

2 tablespoons rice wine (mirin) or dry white wine

1 tablespoon fish sauce

1 teaspoon reduced-salt light soy sauce

2 kaffir lime leaves, optional

1/4 cup/45 g raw unsalted cashews, optional

500 g firm white fish fillets (e.g. ling, flake, Spanish mackerel or gemfish)

1   Place green onions, coriander, ginger, lemon grass, chilli, lime juice, wine, fish and soy sauces, lime leaves and cashews in a deep casserole. Mix to combine. Add fish. Turn to coat. Cover. Marinate in the refrigerator for 1 hour, if possible.

2   Preheat oven to 190°C.

3   Bake fish for 10 minutes or until it just starts to flake when tested with fork.

4   Serve with steamed jasmine rice, steamed snow peas (mangetout) or other steamed Oriental greens of your choice.
Serves 4

898 kilojoules/214 Calories – per serve
6 g total fat; 1 g saturated fat; 595 mg sodium

Ingredient know-how: *Kaffir lime leaves are most commonly available dried. These aromatic, intensely fragrant leaves are used in South-east Asian cooking. Rather than adding flavour, kaffir lime leaves tend to surround the food with an aura and are often the secret behind classic Thai dishes.*

Baked Lime and Lemon Grass Fish

Crab and Pickled Cucumber Salad

mediterraneanmix

Char-grilled Lamb with Vegetable Couscous (page 96)

Char-grilled Lamb with Vegetable Couscous

2 cups/370 g couscous

4 x 125 g lean lamb fillets or loin

3 teaspoons olive oil

finely grated zest and juice of 1 lemon

1 clove garlic, crushed

1 teaspoon cumin seeds

1 eggplant (aubergine), cut into large chunks

1 red pepper, diced

1 bulb fennel, sliced

6 dates, thinly sliced

1/2 cup/125 mL white wine or marsala

3 tablespoons chopped fresh parsley

1   Place 2 cups/500 mL water in a large saucepan. Bring to the boil. Slowly stir in couscous. Remove pan from heat. Cover. Stand for 15 minutes or until liquid is absorbed.

2   Meanwhile, preheat a char-grill pan or barbecue until hot. Brush lamb with a little oil. Place in pan or on barbecue grill. Cook, turning several times, until cooked to your liking. Remove lamb from heat. Place on a plate. Sprinkle with a little of the lemon juice. Cover. Keep warm in a low oven.

3   Heat remaining oil in a nonstick frying pan over a medium heat. Add garlic and cumin seeds. Cook, stirring for 1-2 minutes. Add eggplant and red pepper. Cook for 3-4 minutes or until eggplant starts to soften. Add fennel, dates and wine. Cook, stirring occasionally, for 5-10 minutes or until eggplant is cooked. Add vegetable mixture, parsley, lemon zest and remaining lemon juice to couscous. Toss with a fork to combine. Place saucepan over a low heat. Heat, tossing occasionally, for 4-5 minutes or until heated through.

4   To serve, divide couscous between serving plates. Slice lamb. Arrange on top of couscous. Accompany with lemon wedges.
Serves 4

2539 kilojoules/614 Calories – per serve
9 g total fat; 3 g saturated fat; 115 mg sodium

Lemon and Broccoli Risotto

1 tablespoon olive oil

1 onion, chopped

1 clove garlic, crushed

1 1/2 cups/330 g arborio rice

1 cup/250 mL dry white wine (e.g. sauvignon blanc)

4 cups/1 litre hot chicken stock (page 174)

2 cups/120 g broccoli florets

1/2 cup/30 g chopped fresh parsley

finely grated zest and juice of 1 lemon

crushed black peppercorns

WALNUT PESTO (OPTIONAL)

3 tablespoons walnut pieces, roasted

1 tablespoon green olives, rinsed and drained, chopped

2 teaspoons grated parmesan cheese

2 teaspoons olive oil

2 teaspoons red wine or balsamic vinegar

1   **Pesto:** Place walnuts, olives, parmesan cheese, oil and vinegar in a food processor or blender. Process to make a coarse paste. Set aside.

2   Heat oil in a large heavy-based saucepan over a medium heat. Add onion and garlic. Cook, stirring, for 1-2 minutes or until onion is translucent.

3   Stir in rice. Cook for 1-2 minutes. Add wine. Cook, stirring, until liquid is absorbed. Add 1 cup/250 mL chicken stock and cook, stirring occasionally, until liquid is absorbed. Add another 1 cup/250 mL stock and cook as described above. Continue adding stock 1 cup/250 mL at a time, until all the stock is used and the rice is tender. Add broccoli 2-3 minutes before end of cooking time.

4   Stir in parsley, lemon zest and juice and black pepper to taste. Remove pan from heat. Cover. Stand for 3 minutes. Serve with or without pesto.
Serves 4

1654 kilojoules/403 Calories – per serve (without pesto)
6 g total fat; 1 g saturated fat; 30 mg sodium
1996 kilojoules/486 Calories – per serve (with pesto)
14 g total fat; 2 g saturated fat; 46 mg sodium

Tuna Carpaccio in Witlof Leaves (page 102)

Lemon and Broccoli Risotto

Fettuccine Caprese

500 g fettuccine, linguini or pappardelle (very wide fettuccine)

4 plum or vine-ripened tomatoes, diced

2 cups/60 g fresh basil leaves, shredded

1/3 cup/50 g diced reduced-fat mozzarella or bocconcini cheese

1 tablespoon capers, rinsed and drained

1 tablespoon extra virgin olive oil

1 tablespoon balsamic or red wine vinegar

shaved fresh parmesan cheese, optional

freshly ground black pepper

1   Cook pasta in boiling water in a large saucepan according to packet directions.

2   Place tomatoes, basil, mozzarella cheese, capers, oil and vinegar in a bowl. Toss to combine. Add tomato mixture to hot pasta. Toss.

3   To serve, divide pasta mixture between warm bowls. Scatter with a few parmesan cheese shavings and black pepper to taste. Accompany with a green salad and crusty bread.

Serves 4 as a main meal or 6 as a starter

2206 kilojoules/531 Calories – per serve (as a main meal)
9 g total fat; 2 g saturated fat; 162 mg sodium
1470 kilojoules/354 Calories – per serve (as a starter)
6 g total fat; 2 g saturated fat; 108 mg sodium

Author's note: *One of the simplest, quickest and easiest ways to prepare a pasta meal is to toss a cold, fresh sauce through hot pasta. This recipe based on a classic dish from the beautiful isle of Capri is one of the best, but here are a few more you might like to try.*

Macadamia and coriander pesto: Place 2 cups/60 g fresh coriander leaves, 40 g unsalted macadamia or pistachio pieces, 1 teaspoon minced garlic, 1 tablespoon grated parmesan cheese, 1 tablespoon lemon juice and 2 teaspoons macadamia or olive oil in a food processor. Using the pulse button, process to coarsely chop. Transfer to a bowl. Mix in 1/2 cup/125 g reduced-fat fresh ricotta cheese and 3 tablespoons sliced sun-dried tomatoes. Add to cooked, hot pasta. Toss to combine.

Tuna, olive and feta cheese: Place 220 g drained canned tuna in springwater, 2 tablespoons chopped fresh parsley, a few sliced olives, 60 g reduced-fat and -salt feta or goat's cheese and lemon juice and black pepper to taste in a bowl. Toss to combine. Add to cooked, hot pasta. Toss to combine.

Creamy avocado and ricotta sauce: Place the flesh of 1/2 avocado, 1/2 cup/125 g reduced-fat fresh ricotta cheese, 2 tablespoons low-fat natural yogurt, 1 tablespoon lemon juice and freshly ground black pepper to taste in a food processor. Process until smooth. Spoon over hot, cooked pasta. Scatter with toasted pine nuts and a few lean grilled bacon pieces.

Braised Spanish Meatballs with Risone

3 cups/270 g risone or other pasta of your choice

2 tablespoons chopped fresh parsley or coriander

SPANISH MEATBALLS

700 g lean beef or lamb mince

1 red onion, finely chopped

2 tablespoons finely chopped roasted unsalted almonds

2 tablespoons chopped fresh flat leaf parsley

2 teaspoons paprika

1 teaspoon ground cumin

1 clove garlic, crushed

1 egg, lightly beaten

RED WINE AND TOMATO SAUCE

1 teaspoon olive oil

1 onion, finely chopped

2 teaspoons fennel seeds, optional

1 tablespoon no-added-salt tomato paste

400 g canned no-added-salt diced tomatoes

1 cup/250 mL red wine

**$1/2$ cup/125 mL low-salt beef or chicken stock
(pages 175 and 174)**

1 tablespoon red wine vinegar

1   **Meatballs:** Place mince, onion, almonds, parsley, paprika, cumin, garlic and egg in a bowl. Mix to combine. Shape mixture into small (4-5 cm in diameter) balls. Place on a plate lined with plastic food wrap. Refrigerate until ready to cook.

2   **Sauce:** Heat oil in a heavy-based frying pan with a lid over a medium heat. Add onion. Cook, stirring occasionally, for 4-5 minutes or until translucent. Add fennel seeds. Cook, stirring, for 1 minute. Stir in tomato paste. Cook for 3-4 minutes or until it becomes deep red and develops a rich aroma.

3   Add tomatoes, wine, stock and vinegar. Stirring, bring to the boil. Reduce heat. Carefully add meatballs. Cover. Simmer for 15 minutes. Turn meatballs. Cover. Cook for 10-15 minutes longer or until cooked through. Add a little more stock or water if mixture becomes too thick.

4   Meanwhile, cook pasta in boiling water in a large saucepan according to packet directions.

5   To serve, divide pasta between shallow serving bowls. Spoon over meatballs and sauce. Sprinkle with parsley.
Serves 6

1706 kilojoules/408 Calories – per serve (with pasta)
11 g total fat; 3 g saturated fat; 145 mg sodium
1062 kilojoules/253 Calories – per serve (without pasta)
10 g total fat; 3 g saturated fat; 143 mg sodium

Tapas idea: *Tapas bars are becoming more and more popular all around the world. It's a great way to enjoy good company and a whole range of taste experiences in one meal. These meatballs would be ideal, just skip the risone and serve them with a few other dishes such as Tuna Carpaccio in Witlof Leaves (page 102), Asparagus Parmesan Pastry Spirals and Marinated Grilled Sardines (page 108).*

Rockmelon and Rocket Salad

2 cups/360 g rockmelon, cubes or balls

1 bunch/250 g rocket

$1/4$ cup/60 mL red wine vinegar

1 tablespoon olive oil

freshly ground black pepper

shredded fresh basil

1 tablespoon pine nuts or parmesan cheese shavings

Place rockmelon, rocket, vinegar, oil and black pepper to taste in a bowl. Toss to combine. Scatter with basil and pine nuts or parmesan cheese shavings.
Serves 4

388 kilojoules/94 Calories – per serve
8 g total fat; 1 g saturated fat; 24 mg sodium

Tuna Carpaccio in Witlof Leaves

200 g very fresh tuna, swordfish or kingfish fillets – or use a combination of all three

4 witlof, leaves separated

1 red onion, diced

1 tablespoon capers, rinsed and drained

LIME AND HORSERADISH DRESSING

2 tablespoons olive oil

2 tablespoons lime juice

1 tablespoon sherry or wine vinegar

1 teaspoon horseradish relish

1   Using a very sharp knife, cut fish into paper thin slices – this will be easier to do if you place the fish in the freezer for 10 minutes before slicing – take care not to allow the fish to freeze.

2   Divide fish between the witlof leaves. Scatter each with some chopped onion and a few capers.

3   **Dressing:** Place oil, lime juice, vinegar and horseradish relish in a small bowl. Whisk to combine. Drizzle dressing over fish. Serve immediately with crostini or fresh crusty bread.

Serves 6

513 kilojoules/123 Calories – per serve
8 g total fat; 1 g saturated fat; 97 mg sodium

Author's note: *Use only the freshest fish for this recipe – tell your fishmonger what you are using it for and they will advise you what will be appropriate.*

Red Onion, Red Pepper and Rocket Pizza

2 teaspoons olive oil

4 large red onions, thinly sliced

1 tablespoon balsamic or red wine vinegar

2 tablespoons shredded fresh basil

freshly ground black pepper

1 large or 2 small purchased fresh pizza bases (without sauce)

2 red peppers, roasted, peeled and sliced (page 169)

$1/3$ cup/50 g crumbled reduced-fat and -salt feta cheese

2 tablespoons sliced kalamata olives, rinsed and drained

1 bunch/180 g rocket or baby English spinach leaves

1   Heat oil in a nonstick frying pan over a medium heat. Add onions. Cook, stirring, for 5 minutes or until soft. Reduce heat to low. Cook for 15-20 minutes longer or until onions are caramelised. Remove pan from heat. Stir in vinegar, basil and black pepper to taste.

2   Preheat oven to 240°C. Spread onions over pizza base. Top with red peppers, feta cheese and olives. Bake for 15 minutes or until bases are crisp and golden. Pile rocket on top of pizza. Drizzle with additional balsamic vinegar, if desired. Serve immediately.

Serves 6

570 kilojoules/137 Calories – per serve
4 g total fat; 1 g saturated fat; 163 mg sodium

Roast pumpkin and bocconcini: Spread pizza base with pesto, then top with cooked pumpkin cubes and bocconcini slices. Bake for 15 minutes or until base is crisp and cheese melts.

Spinach and ricotta: Spread pizza base with wholegrain mustard or chutney. Top with shredded, blanched or raw spinach. Cover with spoonfuls of reduced-fat fresh ricotta cheese and season with freshly ground black pepper and grated nutmeg. Bake for 15 minutes or until base is crisp and cheese golden.

Fresh salmon and dill: Cut deboned and skinned salmon fillets in cubes. Toss with fresh herbs of your choice and black pepper to taste. Combine $1/2$ cup/100 g low-fat natural yogurt and 1 tablespoon dijon mustard. Spread over pizza base. Top with salmon cubes, chopped green onions and halved cherry tomatoes. Scatter with a little crumbled reduced-fat and -salt goat's cheese. Bake for 10 minutes or until base is crisp and salmon is just cooked. Serve with low-fat natural yogurt flavoured with fresh chopped dill.

Red Onion, Red Pepper and Rocket Pizza

Chermoula-crusted Chicken on Soft Polenta

750 g skinless chicken breast or thigh fillets, cut into large pieces

¹/₄ cup/60 mL white wine or lemon juice

CHERMOULA

4 tablespoons chopped fresh parsley

4 tablespoons chopped fresh coriander

2 tablespoons minced lemon zest

1 teaspoon ground cumin

1 teaspoon paprika

¹/₂ teaspoon freshly ground black pepper

pinch saffron powder or threads

2 tablespoons lemon juice

1 tablespoon olive oil

SOFT POLENTA

2 cups/500 mL low-salt chicken stock (page 174)

1¹/₂ cups/375 mL water

1 cup/250 mL low-fat milk

2 bay leaves

1 sprig fresh rosemary

1¹/₂ cups/250 g polenta (cornmeal)

1   Lightly spray or brush a flat non-reactive casserole or baking dish with unsaturated oil. Place chicken in a single layer in dish.

2   **Chermoula:** Place parsley, coriander, lemon zest, cumin, paprika, black pepper, saffron, lemon juice and olive oil in a food processor. Using the pulse button, process until just combined – take care not to process until smooth. Spoon chermoula over chicken. Cover. Marinate in the refrigerator for at least 1 hour or overnight.

3   Preheat oven to 180°C. Pour wine over chicken. Bake for 20-30 minutes or until chicken is cooked through.

4   **Polenta:** Meanwhile, place stock, water, milk, bay leaves and rosemary in a large saucepan over a medium heat. Bring to the boil. Remove bay leaves and rosemary. Discard. Gradually stir in polenta. Reduce heat. Simmer, stirring occasionally, for 20 minutes or until mixture thickens and leaves the sides of the pan – add more liquid if the mixture becomes too thick.

5   To serve, spoon polenta onto serving plates. Place chicken on top. Drizzle with some of the cooking juices. Accompany with steamed vegetables such as zucchini (courgettes), red pepper and asparagus.

Serves 6

1387 kilojoules/333 Calories – per serve
7 g total fat; 1 g saturated fat; 90 mg sodium

Tuscan Bread Salad with Poached Trout

2 lemons

4 x 150 g ocean or rainbow trout fillets, skinned and boned

1 sprig fresh rosemary

crushed black peppercorns

¹/₂ cup/125 mL white wine

2 tablespoons balsamic vinegar

2 teaspoons olive oil

TUSCAN BREAD SALAD

4 slices crusty Italian bread

2 teaspoons olive oil

2 teaspoons grated parmesan cheese

3 plum or vine-ripened tomatoes, diced

2 Lebanese cucumbers, diced

1 small red onion, diced

¹/₄ cup/45 g chopped olives, rinsed and drained

1 red pepper, diced or a mixture of red and green peppers

1 tablespoon capers, rinsed and drained

3 tablespoons chopped fresh basil leaves

1   Cut 1 lemon into thin slices. Squeeze the juice from the other. Place fish in a shallow frying pan. Scatter with rosemary leaves and black pepper to taste. Cover with lemon slices. Carefully pour over wine and lemon juice. Cover pan. Poach over a medium heat for 4 minutes or until fish just turns opaque.

2   Place vinegar and oil in a small bowl. Whisk to combine. Set aside.

3   **Salad:** Preheat grill to a medium heat. Grill bread for 3-4 minutes or until lightly toasted on one side. Turn over. Brush second side with oil. Sprinkle with parmesan cheese. Grill for 2-3 minutes longer or until cheese melts and is golden. Cut into 2 cm square croûtons.

4   Place croûtons, tomatoes, cucumbers, onion, olives, red pepper, capers and basil in a bowl. Toss to combine.

5   To serve, divide salad between serving plates. Top with a fish fillet. Drizzle with vinegar mixture.

Serves 4

1891 kilojoules/483 Calories – per serve
15 g total fat; 3 g saturated fat; 450 mg sodium

Tuscan Bread Salad with Poached Trout

Chermoula-crusted Chicken on Soft Polenta

Pumpkin Agnolotti with Rocket Pesto

PUMPKIN AND RICOTTA AGNOLOTTI

2 cups/250 g grated pumpkin

1/2 cup/125 g fresh reduced-fat ricotta cheese

1 tablespoon grated parmesan cheese

1 teaspoon chopped fresh oregano

1 teaspoon ground cumin

1 teaspoon grated fresh ginger

1 egg white, lightly beaten

freshly ground black pepper

30 gow gee or round wonton wrappers

ROCKET PESTO

1 bunch/180 g rocket, leaves chopped – you should have about 2 cups

4 tablespoons chopped fresh mint

1/4 cup/40 g roasted unsalted cashews

1 tablespoon ricotta cheese

1 tablespoon dijon mustard

2 tablespoons red wine vinegar

1   **Agnolotti:** Boil or microwave pumpkin in 2 tablespoons of water until just soft. Drain. Press to remove excess liquid. Place in a bowl. Add ricotta and parmesan cheeses, oregano, cumin, ginger, egg white and black pepper to taste. Mix to combine.

2   Place a few wrappers on a clean, dry surface – cover the rest with a clean damp teatowel to prevent them drying out. Place 1 tablespoon of the pumpkin mixture in the centre of each wrapper, leaving a 1 cm border. Moisten edges of wrapper. Fold in half. Pinch edges to seal. Repeat with remaining wrappers and filling. Place prepared agnolotti in an airtight container lined with greaseproof paper. Store in the refrigerator for at least 1 hour or until ready to cook.

3   **Pesto:** Place rocket, mint, cashews, ricotta cheese, mustard and vinegar in a food processor or blender. Process to make a coarse paste. Transfer to a bowl. Cover. Set aside until ready to serve.

4   Bring a large saucepan of water to the boil. Cook 5-6 agnolotti at a time for 3 minutes or until they float to the surface. Using a slotted spoon, remove agnolotti and place in a warm serving dish. Keep warm while cooking remaining agnolotti.

5   To serve, place agnolotti in shallow bowls. Top with a spoon of pesto.

Serves 6 as a starter or 4 as a main meal

1156 kilojoules/279 Calories – per serve (as a starter)
8 g total fat; 3 g saturated fat; 515 mg sodium
1734 kilojoules/418 Calories – per serve (as a main meal)
12 g total fat; 4 g saturated fat; 772 mg sodium

Asparagus Parmesan Pastry Spirals

6 teaspoons finely grated parmesan cheese

2 teaspoons finely grated lemon zest

1 teaspoon freshly ground black pepper

1 teaspoon paprika, plus extra for dusting

6 sheets filo pastry

12 slices lean, low-fat, reduced-salt turkey ham

12 thick fresh asparagus spears, trimmed

balsamic vinegar

1   Preheat oven to 220°C. Line a baking tray with baking paper or lightly spray or brush with olive oil.

2   Place parmesan cheese, lemon zest, black pepper and paprika in a small bowl. Mix to combine.

3   Lay a sheet of filo pastry on a clean, dry surface. Fold in half lengthwise. Lightly spray or brush with olive oil. Sprinkle with one-sixth of the parmesan mixture. Cut in half lengthwise.

4   Wrap a slice of ham around an asparagus spear. Wind a pastry strip around the outside – working from the base of the asparagus spear, wind in a spiral. Place on prepared baking tray. Repeat with remaining ingredients to make 12 spirals. Dust lightly with extra paprika. Bake for 10-12 minutes or until pastry is golden. Serve with balsamic vinegar for dipping.

Makes 12 spirals

200 kilojoules/48 Calories – per spiral
1 g total fat; less than 1 g saturated fat; 90 mg sodium

Ingredient know-how: *There is now a vast range of specialty hams in delicatessens that are lower in salt and only about 2% fat. The turkey ham I have recommended for this recipe is one such product, but you can use your favourite if you wish. Alternatively, prosciutto could be used, but make sure it's sliced paper thin and only use a little.*

Marinated Grilled Sardines

12 fresh sardines, cleaned, or use fillets if preferred

PARSLEY AND GARLIC MARINADE

1/2 cup/60 g chopped fresh parsley

1 teaspoon crushed black peppercorns

1 clove garlic, crushed

finely grated zest and juice of 1 lemon

2 tablespoons white wine vinegar

1 tablespoon olive oil

1   Preheat a barbecue or grill to a high heat. Place sardines on barbecue or under grill. Cook for 1-2 minutes each side or until crisp and golden. Place sardines in a single layer in a shallow heatproof dish.

2   **Dressing:** Place parsley, black peppercorns, garlic, lemon zest and juice, vinegar and oil in a small saucepan over a medium heat. Bring to the boil. Remove from heat. Pour dressing over sardines. Cover. Marinate for at least 1 hour.

Makes 12 sardines

242 kilojoules/59 Calories – per sardine
5 g total fat; 1 g saturated fat; 69 mg sodium

Author's note: *Instead of the usual process of marinating first, then cooking, these sardines are cooked first then marinated and served cold. If you can't wait, you can eat them as soon as the dressing is poured over and while they are still crackling hot. This recipe is also suitable for other types of fish such as garfish, mullet and mackerel – all of which are loaded with those great Omega 3's.*

southern**spice**

Beef and Pepper Fajitas

500g lean beef steak (e.g. round, sirloin or blade), trimmed of visible fat, cut into thin strips

1 red pepper, cut into thin strips

1 green pepper, cut into thin strips

1 yellow pepper, cut into thin strips

1 onion, sliced

3 tomatoes, diced

6 large flour tortillas

LIME AND PAWPAW MARINADE

2 garlic cloves, crushed

1 tablespoon ground cumin

1/2 teaspoon crushed black peppercorns

1/2 cup/125 mL pawpaw nectar

juice of 1 lime

dash tabasco sauce or 1 teaspoon chilli powder

HOT YOGURT SAUCE

2 tablespoons chopped green onions or chives

3 tablespoons low-fat natural yogurt

juice of 1 lime

dash tabasco sauce

1 **Marinade:** Place garlic, cumin, black peppercorns, pawpaw nectar, lime juice and tabasco sauce to taste in a glass or ceramic bowl. Add beef. Toss to combine. Cover. Marinate in the refrigerator for at least 1 hour.

2 **Sauce:** Place green onions, yogurt, lime juice and tabasco sauce to taste in a small bowl. Mix to combine. Cover. Refrigerate until ready to use.

3 Heat a large nonstick frying pan over a high heat. Lightly spray or brush with unsaturated oil. Drain beef. Add to pan. Stir-fry for 5 minutes or until cooked to your liking. Remove meat from pan. Keep warm.

4 Add red, green and yellow peppers and onion to pan. Stir-fry until peppers are tender crisp. Return meat to pan. Toss.

5 Meanwhile, wrap tortillas in aluminium foil. Heat in a low oven for 5 minutes. Alternatively, wrap in a clean cloth or absorbent kitchen paper. Heat in the microwave on HIGH (100%) for 1 1/2-2 minutes. Place meat mixture down the centre of each tortilla. Top with tomato. Drizzle with sauce. Roll up. Serve with a green salad.

Serves 6

1192 kilojoules/285 Calories – per fajita
6 g total fat; 2 g saturated fat; 334 mg sodium

Chilli Turkey Pot Pie

1 quantity Polenta Pastry (page 168)

1 teaspoon paprika

CHILLI TURKEY FILLING

2 teaspoons unsaturated oil

1 onion, finely diced

1 stalk celery, sliced

1 clove garlic, crushed

2 teaspoons chilli powder

2 teaspoons ground cumin

1 teaspoon fresh oregano

2 tablespoons no-added-salt tomato paste

500 g lean turkey or chicken mince or thinly sliced, skinless breast or thigh meat

425 g canned no-added-salt diced tomatoes, undrained

440 g cooked or canned red kidney or pinto beans, rinsed and drained

1 1/2 cups/290 g canned no-added-salt sweet corn kernels, rinsed and drained, or kernels from 1 cob sweet corn, cooked

3 tablespoons chopped fresh coriander

1 Preheat oven to 180°C. Make up pastry as directed. Wrap in plastic food wrap. Chill until required. Lightly spray or brush a large deep casserole dish with unsaturated oil.

2 **Filling:** Heat oil in a large nonstick frying pan over a medium heat. Add onion, celery and garlic. Cook, stirring occasionally, for 5 minutes or until vegetables are soft. Stir in chilli powder, cumin, oregano and tomato paste. Cook for 3-4 minutes or until it becomes deep red and develops a rich aroma.

3 Add mince. Cook, stirring, for 5 minutes. Stir in tomatoes. Bring to simmering. Cover. Simmer for 10-12 minutes or until mixture reduces and thickens slightly. Mix in beans, sweet corn and coriander. Spoon mixture into prepared dish. Cool.

4 Brush edge of dish with water. Roll out pastry to 3 cm larger than dish. Lay over filling. Seal edges to dish. Crimp edges. Dust top of pie with paprika. Bake for 20-25 minutes or until filling is bubbling and pastry is crisp and golden.

Serves 6

2064 kilojoules/496 Calories – per serve (with pastry topping, using canned beans)
13 g total fat; 2 g saturated fat; 556 mg sodium
998 kilojoules/238 Calories – per serve (without pastry topping, using canned beans)
5 g total fat; 1 g saturated fat; 391 mg sodium

Cook's tip: *Use this filling for burritos, tacos or baked potatoes.*

Quinoa, Corn and Black Bean Salad

1 cup/200 g quinoa

2 red banana peppers, roasted (page 169), flesh diced

1 cup/180 g cooked or canned black kidney (turtle) or pinto beans

1 cup/200 g drained, canned no-added-salt sweet corn kernels

1/2 cup/65 g diced white or red radish or jicama

1/2 cup/25 g chopped fresh coriander

1 tablespoon finely chopped fresh or canned jalapeño or anaheim chilli

1 green onion, chopped

LIME VINAIGRETTE

1 teaspoon grated lime zest

1/2 teaspoon brown sugar

2 tablespoons lime juice

2 tablespoons raspberry vinegar

1 tablespoon sherry

2 teaspoons unsaturated oil

2 teaspoons horseradish cream

dash tabasco sauce

1 Rinse quinoa thoroughly under cold running water. Drain well. Place 2 cups/500 mL water in a saucepan. Bring to the boil. Stir in quinoa. Reduce heat. Cover. Simmer for 10-15 minutes or until water is absorbed and quinoa is transparent. Drain. Cool.

2 **Vinaigrette:** Place lime zest, sugar, lime juice, vinegar, sherry, oil, horseradish cream and tabasco sauce in a screwtop jar. Shake well to combine. Set aside.

3 Place prepared quinoa, peppers, beans, sweet corn, radish, coriander, chilli and green onion in a bowl. Spoon over dressing. Toss to combine.

Serves 6 as a side dish

849 kilojoules/205 Calories – per serve (using fresh cooked beans)
3 g total fat; less than 1 g saturated fat; 53 mg sodium

Ingredient know-how: *Quinoa (pronounced 'keen-wa') is a grain with an interesting crunchy texture and delicate flavour. It is delicious in salads or use it as you would rice. Quinoa is high in calcium, protein and fibre and low in fat. Rinse before using to remove the bitter flavour. It is available from most health food stores, delicatessens and some supermarkets.*

Spicy Soft Fish Tacos

400 g tuna, salmon or swordfish steaks, cut 2-3 cm thick, skinned and boned

juice of 1 lime

freshly ground black pepper

8 small corn tortillas

2 cups/90 g shredded lettuce

2 large tomatoes, diced

2 green onions, thinly sliced

purchased taco sauce, optional – look for varieties with reduced-salt and no-added-fat

AVOCADO AND CORIANDER SALSA

1 avocado, stoned, peeled and chopped

2 tablespoons chopped fresh coriander

dash tabasco or a pinch of chilli powder

1 Heat a nonstick frying pan or grill until hot. Lightly spray or brush fish with olive oil. Place in pan or under grill. Cook for 3-4 minutes each side or until flesh just starts to flake when tested with a fork. Transfer fish to a heatproof bowl. Break into pieces. Sprinkle with a little of the lime juice and season with black pepper to taste. Cover. Keep warm.

2 Heat a clean nonstick frying pan over a medium heat. Dry-fry 1-2 tortillas at a time for 1 minute each side or until brown spots appear. Remove from pan. Cover with aluminium foil. Keep warm. Alternatively, wrap in a clean cloth or absorbent kitchen paper. Heat in the microwave on HIGH (100%) for 1 1/2-2 minutes.

3 **Salsa:** Place avocado, coriander, tabasco sauce to taste and remaining lime juice in a bowl. Toss. Set aside.

4 Add lettuce, tomatoes and green onions to fish mixture. Toss.

5 To serve, top warm tortillas with avocado mixture, fish, mixture and taco sauce to taste. Fold and eat in your hands.

Serves 4

2170 kilojoules/522 Calories – per taco
16 g total fat; 3 g saturated fat; 620 mg sodium

Author's note: *The Coriander Pesto served with the Grilled Tequila Pork is a delicious alternative to the Avocado Salsa.*

Quinoa, Corn and Black Bean Salad

Spicy Soft Fish Tacos

Wild Rice Jambalaya

1 cup/190 g wild rice

2 teaspoons olive oil

$^{1}/_{2}$ cup/60 g chopped celery

$^{1}/_{2}$ cup/80 g diced red pepper

$^{1}/_{2}$ cup/80 g diced green or yellow pepper

1 onion, chopped

1 rasher lean bacon, trimmed of visible fat or 1 sliced smoked salmon, finely diced

2 cloves garlic, crushed

2 tablespoons no-added-salt tomato paste

1 tablespoon fresh thyme or $^{1}/_{2}$ teaspoon dried thyme

1 cup/200 g long grain white rice

1 small Mexican chilli, seeded and finely chopped or $^{1}/_{2}$ teaspoon cayenne pepper

1 tablespoon chopped canned pimento or jalapeño chilli, optional

400 g canned no-added-salt tomatoes, drained and chopped

1$^{1}/_{2}$ cups/375 mL low-salt chicken stock (page 174)

1 cup/250 mL dry white wine

700 g peeled, uncooked medium prawns, deveined

3 tablespoons chopped fresh coriander or parsley

8 Grilled Chilli Sopaipillas (recipe follows), optional

1   Place wild rice in a saucepan. Pour over water to cover. Bring to the boil. Boil for 5 minutes. Remove pan from heat. Cover tightly. Steam for 30 minutes. Drain.

2   Heat oil in a large, high-sided nonstick frying pan. Add celery, red and green peppers, onion, bacon and garlic. Cook, stirring, for 3-4 minutes or until vegetables are soft. Stir in tomato paste and thyme. Cook for 2 minutes.

3   Add prepared wild rice, white rice, chilli, pimento, tomatoes, stock and wine. Bring to the boil. Reduce heat. Simmer for 15-20 minutes or until rice is tender, but still firm in the centre.

4   Add prawns. Cook, stirring occasionally, for 7-8 minutes or until prawns are cooked.

5   To serve, spoon jambalaya into warm large bowls. Scatter with coriander and accompany with sopaipillas or crusty bread.

Serves 8

2073 kilojoules/500 Calories – per serve (with sopaipillas)
3 g total fat; less than 1 g saturated fat; 468 mg sodium
1321 kilojoules/317 Calories – per serve (without sopaipillas)
8 g total fat; less than 1 g saturated fat; 441 mg sodium

Grilled Chilli Sopaipillas

1$^{1}/_{2}$ cups/185 g plain or wholemeal flour

1 teaspoon baking powder

$^{1}/_{2}$ teaspoon cayenne pepper or chilli powder

$^{1}/_{2}$ cup/125 mL low-fat milk, scalded and cooled to room temperature

$^{1}/_{4}$ cup/60 mL warm water

1 tablespoon no-added-salt tomato paste

3 tablespoons finely chopped fresh chives or coriander

$^{1}/_{2}$ teaspoon garlic powder

1   Place flour, baking powder and cayenne pepper in a food processor. Process briefly to sift. Combine milk and water. With machine running, slowly add milk mixture. Process until mixture forms a sticky dough. Turn dough onto a floured surface. Knead until smooth and springy. Wrap in plastic food wrap. Rest for 15 minutes.

2   Divide dough into four portions. Roll each out to form a 10 x 25 cm rectangle. Spread with tomato paste, leaving a 1.5 cm border. Sprinkle with chives and garlic powder. Starting at the long edge, roll up each rectangle like a Swiss roll, then shape into a coil (like a snail shell). Seal edges with water. Using a floured rolling pin, roll out each coil to form a 5 mm thick circle.

3   Heat a nonstick frying pan over a medium heat. Lightly spray or brush with unsaturated oil. Cook sopaipillas until golden and puffy. Turn over. Cook until brown on other side.

Makes 4 sopaipillas

753 kilojoules/183 Calories – per sopaipilla
1 g total fat; less than 1 g saturated fat; 27 mg sodium

Cook's tip: *Serve sopaipillas hot with any meal or soup instead of bread. Alternatively, for a light meal, top with ingredients such as tomato, goat's cheese, herbs or avocado. Finish in a hot oven or under the grill.*

Chicken and Corn Quesadillas with Salsa

2 teaspoons unsaturated oil

3 skinless chicken breast fillets, trimmed of visible fat, cut into thin strips

1 cup/200 g fresh cooked or canned no-added-salt, rinsed and drained, sweet corn kernels

2 green onions or shallots, chopped

1/2 cup/25 g chopped fresh coriander

1 tablespoon lime or lemon juice

2 tablespoons purchased taco sauce

12 large flour tortillas

1 cup/150 g grated reduced-fat mozzarella cheese

1 cup/50 g shredded salad greens of your choice (e.g. radicchio, rocket or butter lettuce)

AVOCADO AND TOMATO SALSA

1 avocado, stoned, peeled and diced

1 tablespoon lime or lemon juice

1/2 red onion, diced

1 tomato, diced

2 tablespoons chopped fresh coriander

tabasco or chilli sauce

1 **Salsa:** Place avocado, lime juice, onion, tomato, coriander and tabasco sauce to taste in a bowl. Toss. Cover. Set aside until ready to serve.

2 Heat oil in a large nonstick frying pan over a medium heat. Add chicken, sweet corn and green onions. Cook, stirring, for 5-6 minutes or until chicken is cooked.

3 Stir in coriander, lime juice and taco sauce. Cook for 1-2 minutes. Remove chicken mixture from pan. Keep warm.

4 Wipe pan clean with absorbent kitchen paper. Heat over a medium-high heat. Working with one tortilla at a time, sprinkle tortilla with 2 tablespoons cheese then top with salad greens and one-sixth of the chicken mixture. Cover with a second tortilla. Press edges to seal.

5 Place quesadillas in pan. Cook, pressing gently with an egg slice to spread filling – do not press too hard or the filling will spill out the sides – for 2 minutes or until brown. Turn over. Cook for 1-2 minutes longer or until filling is heated through. Keep cooked quesadillas warm in a low oven while cooking the remainder. To serve, cut into wedges and accompany with salsa.

Makes 6

2549 kilojoules/614 Calories – per quesadilla (with salsa)
21 g total fat; 6 g saturated fat; 826 mg sodium
2175 kilojoules/523 Calories – per quesadilla (without salsa)
12 g total fat; 4 g saturated fat; 823 mg sodium

Author's note: *Quesadillas are the Mexican equivalent of the toasted sandwich – they can be as simple or exotic as you want. They can be stacked or folded – it's just up to your imagination.*

Grilled Tequila Pork with Coriander Pesto

1 teaspoon grated lime or lemon zest

2 tablespoons tequila

1 tablespoon lime or pineapple juice

2 teaspoons no-added-salt worcestershire sauce

4 x 125 g pork leg steaks, trimmed of visible fat

CORIANDER PESTO

1 cup/50 g chopped fresh coriander

1/3 cup/50 g unsalted cashews

2 fresh jalapeño chillies

1 teaspoon ground coriander

2 tablespoons white wine or champagne vinegar

1 tablespoon lime juice

1 tablespoon unsaturated oil

1 tablespoon low-fat natural yogurt or reduced-fat sour cream, optional

1 Combine lime zest, tequila, lime juice and worcestershire sauce in a shallow dish. Add pork. Turn to coat all surfaces. Cover. Marinate in the refrigerator for 10-15 minutes.

2 **Pesto:** Place fresh coriander, cashews, chillies, ground coriander, vinegar, lime juice, oil and yogurt in a food processor or blender. Process to make a coarse paste.

3 Heat a char-grill pan or barbecue to very hot. Add pork. Cook for 3-4 minutes each side or until cooked through.

4 Serve pork topped with a spoonful of pesto and accompanied by steamed rice and a salad of fresh tomatoes and cucumber.

Serves 4

1196 kilojoules/286 Calories – per serve (with pesto)
13 g total fat; 2 g saturated fat; 179 mg sodium
656 kilojoules/155 Calories – per serve (without pesto)
2 g total fat; 1 g saturated fat; 171 mg sodium

Chicken and Corn Quesadillas with Salsa

Grilled Tequila Pork with Coriander Pesto

Louisiana Crusted Chicken with Green Rice

3 small corn tortillas, cut into wedges

1 tablespoon mild paprika

1 tablespoon cornflour

2 teaspoons cajun spice mix (see note at end of recipe)

2 egg whites, beaten

1 tablespoon lime juice

1 teaspoon honey

4 x 125 g skinless chicken breast fillets, trimmed of visible fat

1 quantity Green Rice (recipe follows)

1 quantity Fresh Caribbean Tomato Salsa (page 170)

1   Preheat oven to 220°C.

2   Place tortilla wedges on a baking tray. Bake for 10 minutes or until crisp. Place tortillas and paprika in a food processor. Using the pulse, process to make a coarse meal. Alternatively, place tortillas and paprika in a plastic food bag. Crush using a rolling pin. Transfer to a shallow dish. Set aside.

3   Place cornflour and cajun spice mix in a plastic food bag. Set aside. Place egg whites, lime juice and honey in a shallow dish. Mix to combine. Set aside.

4   Using a meat mallet, pound chicken until 2 mm thick – about the thickness of a schnitzel. Alternatively, ask your butcher to do this for you. Place chicken in bag with cornflour mixture. Shake to coat. Shake off excess mixture. Dip into egg whites. Press in tortilla crumbs to coat and make a firm crust. Place chicken on a plate lined with plastic food wrap. Refrigerate for 10-15 minutes or until ready to cook – this firms the crust and helps it stay on during cooking.

5   Lightly spray or brush a nonstick frying pan with olive oil and heat to medium-high. Add chicken. Cook for 4-5 minutes each side, or until brown and cooked through. Serve with Green Rice, salsa and a fresh green salad.

Serves 4

2308 kilojoules/554 Calories – per serve (with rice and salsa)
4 g total fat; 1 g saturated fat; 340 mg sodium
1098 kilojoules/262 Calories – per serve (without rice and salsa)
4 g total fat; 1 g saturated fat; 286 mg sodium

Ingredient know-how: *Cajun spice mix, sometimes called blackened fish or chicken spice is available from most supermarkets or specialty spice shops. The commercially available mixes are usually fairly high in salt, so you may want to make your own. For a recipe see Cajun-crusted Fish (page 52). While flour tortillas can be used for this recipe, the corn tortillas are more flavoursome and texture is crisper.*

Green Rice

1 cup/50 g chopped fresh coriander

1 fresh mild green chilli, seeded and chopped

1 clove garlic, crushed

2¹/₂ cups/600 mL low-salt vegetable stock (page 175)

1¹/₂ cups/280 g long grain rice

1   Place coriander, chilli, garlic and ¹/₂ cup/125 mL of the stock in a blender. Purée.

2   Heat a large, heavy-based saucepan over medium heat. Add rice. Cook, swirling pan, for 30 seconds or until rice is lightly toasted. Stir in coriander mixture and remaining stock. Bring to the boil. Reduce heat. Cover. Simmer for 15-20 minutes or until rice is tender.

Serves 4

1142 kilojoules/276 Calories – per serve
1 g total fat; less than 1 g saturated fat; 34 mg sodium

Louisiana Crusted Chicken served with Green Rice

comfort**food**

Steak and Oyster Pot Pie

750 g lean round or topside steak, trimmed of visible fat, diced

1/2 cup/60 g flour, seasoned with black pepper

1 tablespoon olive oil

1 onion, diced

1 large carrot, chopped

1 parsnip, chopped

2 stalks celery, chopped

1/4 cup/60 mL no-added-salt tomato paste

1 cup/250 mL red wine

1 cup/250 mL low-salt beef stock (page 175)

1/2 cup/125 mL strong coffee

1 teaspoon no-added-salt worcestershire sauce

12 fresh oysters or 2 x 85 g canned smoked oysters, rinsed and drained

3 tablespoons chopped fresh parsley

2 tablespoons cornflour blended with 1/4 cup/60 mL water

1/2 quantity Ricotta Pastry (page 168)

1 Place meat and flour in a plastic food bag. Toss to coat.

2 Heat half the oil in a large nonstick frying pan over a medium heat. Add onion, carrot, parsnip and celery. Cook, stirring, for 3 minutes or until vegetables are soft. Remove vegetables from pan. Set aside.

3 Add remaining oil to pan and heat. Shake excess flour from meat. Add to pan. Cook, turning several times, until brown on all sides. Stir in tomato paste. Cook for 3-4 minutes or until it becomes deep red and develops a rich aroma. Return vegetables to pan. Add wine, stock, coffee and worcestershire sauce. Cover. Cook over a low heat, stirring occasionally, for 20 minutes.

4 Stir in oysters, parsley and cornflour mixture. Cook, stirring, for 2-3 minutes or until mixture thickens. Remove pan from heat. Cool.

5 Preheat oven to 190°C. Transfer meat mixture to a deep pie dish. Roll out pastry. Place over meat mixture. Bake for 20 minutes or until pastry is golden. Alternatively, bake in individual pie dishes. Serve with a green salad and crusty bread.
Serves 6

1112 kilojoules/265 Calories – per serve (using fresh oysters)
9 g total fat; 3 g saturated fat; 217 mg sodium

Pork Medallions with Winter Fruits

1 red delicious apple, diced

1 pear, diced

1/2 cup/125 mL dry white wine

1/2 cup/125 mL low-salt chicken stock (page 174)

100 g dried fruit of choice (e.g. apricots, peaches, pears, prunes – go for a colourful mix)

1 teaspoon ground cinnamon

1 tablespoon olive oil

500 g lean pork loin, trimmed of visible fat, cut into 5 mm thick medallions

2 tablespoons brandy

1/4 cup/30 g chopped roasted unsalted walnuts, optional

1 Place apple, pear, wine and stock in a saucepan. Bring to simmering. Cook until fruit is soft. Stir in dried fruit and cinnamon. Cook until fruit is plump. Remove pan from heat. Cool.

2 Heat oil in a nonstick frying pan over a high heat. Add pork. Cook, turning several times, until browned on all sides. Remove pork from pan. Pour brandy into pan and add a little of the cooking liquid from the fruit. Cook over a medium heat, stirring constantly, to deglaze pan. Stir in fruit mixture. Cook until heated through.

3 Return pork to pan. Cook, stirring occasionally, for 4-5 minutes or until pork is cooked to your liking. Scatter with walnuts.

4 Serve with cooked pasta, rice or lima beans and steamed green vegetables of your choice.
Serves 4

1567 kilojoules/374 Calories – per serve
12 g total fat; 2 g saturated fat; 106 mg sodium

Italian Meatloaf

500 g lean beef mince

3/4 cup/75 g rolled oats

1/2 cup/60 g grated sweet potato – or try carrot, parsnip, pumpkin or white potato

1/4 cup/40 g coarsely grated red onion

2 tablespoons chopped fresh herbs (e.g. parsley or basil)

2 teaspoons brown sugar

1 teaspoon dried oregano or thyme

2 eggs

1 egg white

2 tablespoons no-added-salt tomato paste

freshly ground black pepper

CHEESE AND TOMATO FILLING

1/2 cup/75 g crumbled reduced-fat and -salt feta cheese

1/2 cup/80 g chopped sun-dried tomatoes, rehydrated in boiling water and drained

TOMATO SAUCE

1/4 cup/60 mL red wine or port

1/4 cup/60 mL no-added-salt tomato sauce

1 teaspoon no-added-salt worcestershire sauce

1　Preheat oven to 180°C. Lightly spray or brush a 13 x 21 cm loaf tin with unsaturated oil.

2　Place mince, rolled oats, sweet potato, onion, fresh herbs, sugar, oregano, eggs, egg white, tomato paste and black pepper to taste in a bowl. Mix to combine. Press half of the mixture into the prepared tin. Cover evenly with feta cheese and sun-dried tomatoes. Top with remaining meat mixture.

3　**Sauce:** Place wine and tomato and worcestershire sauces in a small bowl. Mix to combine. Pour sauce over meatloaf. Bake for 1 hour or until cooked. To test if meatloaf is cooked through, insert a knife into the centre and press to see if any juices escape.

4　Serve hot with mashed potato and steamed green vegetables of your choice or cold with salads or as a sandwich filling.

Makes a 13 x 21cm loaf – cuts into 20 slices

286 kilojoules/68 Calories – per 1 cm slice
2 g total fat; 1 g saturated fat; 47 mg sodium

Cook's tip: *For something different, serve with horseradish-flavoured mash. To make, mash cooked potatoes with horseradish relish and black pepper to taste; use buttermilk or low-fat natural yogurt to achieve the desired consistency.*

Braised Veal with Risone and Wild Rice

500 g lean veal fillet or schnitzel, trimmed of visible fat and pounded until flat

1 tablespoon olive oil

1 onion, diced

1 stalk celery, sliced

2 tablespoons no-added-salt tomato paste

1 cup/250 mL canned no-added-salt diced tomatoes or passata (concentrated tomato purée)

1 carrot, cut into thin strips

1/2 cup/60 g sultanas

1 cup/250 mL white wine

1 cup/40 g shredded spinach or sliced zucchini (courgettes)

2 tablespoons fresh parsley or basil

1 cup/190 g wild rice

2 cups/250 g risone pasta

1　Cut veal into long wide strips – allow about 4 strips per serve.

2　Heat oil in a heavy-based nonstick saucepan over a medium heat. Add onion and celery. Cook, stirring, for 2-3 minutes or until soft.

3　Add meat. Cook, stirring, until brown on all sides. Stir in tomato paste. Cook for 3-4 minutes or until it becomes deep red and develops a rich aroma.

4　Stir in tomatoes, carrot, sultanas and wine. Bring to simmering. Cover. Simmer over a low heat for 20 minutes or until meat is nearly cooked and sauce starts to thicken. If the mixture becomes too thick, add a little more wine or water. Stir in spinach and parsley. Cook for 5 minutes.

5　Meanwhile, cook rice in boiling water for 10-15 minutes or until grains are just starting to curl. Stir in pasta. Cook for 10 minutes or until rice is tender and pasta is *al dente*.

6　To serve, divide rice mixture between serving plates, spoon over braised veal and accompany with mashed pumpkin and steamed green vegetables of your choice.

Serves 4

2799 kilojoules/673 Calories – per serve (using no-added-salt tomatoes)
8 g total fat; 1 g saturated fat; 172 mg sodium

Italian Meatloaf

Braised Veal with Risone and Wild Rice

Three Potato Pancakes

200 g potatoes, scrubbed and grated

200 g white sweet potato, peeled and grated

200 g orange sweet potato, peeled and grated

1 red onion, finely chopped

2 tablespoons plain flour

2 tablespoons chopped fresh parsley or basil

1 tablespoon grated parmesan cheese

2 eggs, lightly beaten

freshly ground black pepper

1 quantity Roast Lamb Hash (recipe follows)

1   Place potatoes, sweet potatoes, onion, flour, parsley, parmesan cheese, eggs and black pepper to taste in a bowl. Mix to combine.

2   Lightly spray or brush a nonstick frying pan with olive oil. Heat over a high heat. Take 2-3 tablespoons of mixture and place in pan. Press down slightly to form 'pancakes'. Cook for 4-5 minutes each side or until golden. Remove to a baking dish, lined with absorbent kitchen paper. Keep warm in a low oven. Repeat with remaining mixture. Cook 3-4 pancakes at a time or as many as will fit in the pan.

3   Serve with Roast Lamb Hash or with a spoonful of herb-flavoured Yogurt Cheese (page 176), fresh tomato sauce and a green salad.

Serves 4

1603 kilojoules/384 Calories – per serve (with hash)
10 g total fat; 3 g saturated fat; 208 mg sodium
1041 kilojoules/250 Calories – per serve (with Yogurt Cheese)
4 g total fat; 1 g saturated fat; 187 mg sodium

Cook's tip: *These pancakes are an adaptation of the traditional latkes. You could also use the mixture to make a dish similar to a rosti by making one large pancake and finishing under the grill. If you don't have time to stand over the frying pan, place mounds of mixture on a greased baking tray and bake at 180°C for 15 minutes. Turn over and cook for 8 minutes longer.*

Roast Lamb Hash

1 teaspoon unsaturated oil

1 small onion, diced

1 stalk celery, chopped

2 tablespoons no-added-salt tomato paste

400 g lean roast lamb, cut into bite-sized cubes

425 g canned no-added-salt diced tomatoes

2 tablespoons chopped fresh parsley or basil

freshly ground black pepper

1   Heat oil in a saucepan over a medium heat. Add onion and celery. Cook, stirring, for 2-3 minutes or until soft.

2   Stir in tomato paste and cook for 3-4 minutes or until it becomes deep red and develops a rich aroma.

3   Add lamb, tomatoes, parsley and black pepper to taste. Cook, stirring occasionally, for 5-10 minutes or until meat is heated and sauce reduces and thickens.

4   Serve with Three Potato Pancakes.

Serves 4

1603 kilojoules/384 Calories – per serve (with pancakes)
10 g total fat; 3 g saturated fat; 208 mg sodium
662 kilojoules/157 Calories – per serve (without pancakes)
5 g total fat; 2 g saturated fat; 99 mg sodium

Author's note: *This is a very simple home-style comfort dish. If you want to jazz it up a bit, you might like to add some chopped artichoke hearts, semi-dried tomatoes, roasted peppers or other gourmet vegetables of your choice and maybe a splash of wine. It is also delicious served with plain mashed potato.*

Roast Lamb Hash served with Three Potato Pancakes

Middle Eastern Chicken Pasties

1 quantity Ricotta Pastry (page 168)

milk

CHICKEN AND VEGETABLE FILLING

1 teaspoon olive oil

1 small red onion, diced

1 stalk celery, diced

1 teaspoon ground cumin

$1/2$ teaspoon dry mustard

$1^1/4$ cups/200 g skinless shredded cooked chicken

$1/2$ cup/70 g grated zucchini (courgette) or chopped green pepper

$1/2$ cup/30-60 g additional vegetables of your choice (e.g. chopped spinach or grated pumpkin)

2 tablespoons currants or sultanas

1 tablespoon chopped fresh parsley or oregano

$1/4$ cup/45 g low-fat natural yogurt

1 tablespoon chutney

2 tablespoons couscous

1 teaspoon grated lemon zest

2 teaspoons lemon juice

1   **Filling:** Heat oil in a nonstick frying pan over a medium heat. Add onion, celery, cumin and mustard. Cook, stirring, for 2-3 minutes or until soft and fragrant.

2   Add chicken, zucchini, additional vegetables, currants, parsley, yogurt and chutney. Cook, stirring occasionally, for 5-7 minutes. Remove pan from heat. Stir in couscous and lemon zest and juice. Cool.

3   Preheat oven to 190°C. Lightly spray or brush a baking tray with unsaturated oil or line with nonstick baking paper.

4   To assemble, roll out pastry to 2 mm thick and, using a bread and butter plate as a guide, cut out four rounds. Place one-quarter of the filling on one half of each round, leaving a 1 cm border around the edge. Brush edge with milk or water. Fold uncovered half over filling, pressing edges to seal. Using a fork, prick pastry, several times. Place on a prepared baking tray. Brush with milk. Bake for 20 minutes or until pastry is crisp and golden.

Makes 4 pasties

2283 kilojoules/549 Calories – per pastie
18 g total fat; 4 g saturated fat; 622 mg sodium

Cook's tip: *If you're pushed for time, just mix some curry powder or your favourite spice paste to taste with the cooked chicken, yogurt, chutney, currants and grated vegetables as the filling. You could also wrap the filling in Lavash bread or filo pastry instead of making your own pastry. Tuna is an easy and tasty alternative to the chicken.*

Slow-cooked Lamb and Macadamias

600 g boneless leg lamb, trimmed of visible fat, cut in 3 cm cubes

$1/3$ cup/50 g raisins

150 mL evaporated skim milk

SPICY YOGURT MARINADE

1 white onion, diced

$1/3$ cup/50 g ground unsalted macadamias

1-2 cm piece fresh ginger, chopped

125 g low-fat natural yogurt

2 teaspoons lime or lemon juice

3 teaspoons ground coriander

2 teaspoons ground cardamom

$1/2$ teaspoon freshly ground black pepper

1   **Marinade:** Place onion, macadamias, ginger, yogurt and lime juice in a food processor. Process to combine. Stir in coriander, cardamom and black pepper.

2   Place lamb in a non-reactive dish. Pour over marinade. Toss to coat. Cover. Marinate in the refrigerator overnight.

3   Transfer meat mixture to a heavy-based saucepan. Stir in raisins and evaporated milk. Place pan over a medium heat. Bring to simmering. Reduce heat to low. Cover. Cook, stirring occasionally for $1^1/2$ hours.

4   Remove cover. Cook, stirring occasionally, for 30-40 minutes longer or until meat is tender and sauce is thick. Add a little water during cooking, if necessary.

5   Serve with cooked rice and steamed vegetables of your choice.

Serves 4

1509 kilojoules/360 Calories – per serve
15 g total fat; 4 g saturated fat; 186 mg sodium

Baked Ratatouille and Penne
(page 132)

Slow-cooked Lamb and
Macadamias

Middle Eastern Chicken Pasties

Baked Ratatouille and Penne

3 cups/500 g cooked penne or other short pasta of your choice

1 medium eggplant (aubergine), cut into 3 cm cubes

2 large zucchini (courgettes), cut into 3 cm cubes

2 tablespoons olive oil

1 onion, chopped

1 red pepper, cut into 3 cm cubes

1 green pepper, cut into 3 cm cubes

5 plum tomatoes, diced or 12 cherry tomatoes, halved

2 cloves garlic, crushed

1 teaspoon chopped fresh thyme or $1/2$ teaspoon dried thyme

$1/2$ cup/125 g reduced-fat fresh ricotta cheese

2 tablespoons finely chopped basil

1   Preheat oven to 180°C. Lightly spray or brush a deep casserole dish with unsaturated oil. Place penne in the base of the casserole dish.

2   Place eggplant and zucchini in a colander over a bowl. Sprinkle with salt. Stand for 15-20 minutes. Rinse under cold running water. Drain. Pat dry with absorbent kitchen paper.

3   Heat oil in a large nonstick frying pan over a medium heat. Add onion and red and green peppers. Cook, stirring, for 2-3 minutes or until vegetables start to soften. Add eggplant and zucchini. Cook for 2-3 minutes. Remove vegetable mixture from pan. Set aside.

4   Add tomatoes, garlic and thyme to pan. Cook until tomatoes start to collapse. Return vegetable mixture to pan. Mix to combine. Spoon vegetable mixture over penne in casserole dish – as you spoon in the vegetable mixture, push the first few spoonfuls into the pasta. Top vegetable mixture with spoonfuls of ricotta cheese. Scatter with basil. Bake for 5-10 minutes or until ricotta cheese starts to brown.

Serves 6

937 kilojoules/226 Calories – per serve
9 g total fat; 2 g saturated fat; 54 mg sodium

Mussels with Tomatoes and Wine

1 kg fresh mussels, scrubbed and beards removed

1 shallot, chopped

1 cup/250 mL dry white wine

chopped fresh chives

TOMATO AND SMOKED SALMON SAUCE

2 teaspoons olive oil

2 cloves garlic, crushed

2 shallots, chopped

2-3 slices smoked salmon, sliced into thin strips

1 red pepper, sliced

1 tablespoon no-added-salt tomato paste

425 g canned no-added-salt diced tomatoes

2 tablespoons chopped fresh parsley

1   **Sauce:** Heat oil in a nonstick frying pan over a medium heat. Add garlic and shallots. Cook, stirring, for 1-2 minutes. Add salmon and red pepper. Cook, stirring, for 3 minutes. Stir in tomato paste. Cook for 3-4 minutes or until it becomes deep red and develops a rich aroma. Add tomatoes. Cook, stirring, for 5 minutes or until mixture starts to thicken. Stir in parsley. Keep warm.

2   Meanwhile, place mussels, shallot and wine in a large saucepan over a high heat. Cover. Bring to the boil. Reduce heat. Cook for 5 minutes or until mussels open. Discard any mussels that do not open after 5 minutes cooking.

3   Add sauce to mussels. Toss to combine.

4   To serve, divide mixture between deep bowls. Scatter with chives. Accompany with crusty bread and a glass of red wine.

Serves 4

1232 kilojoules/346 Calories – per serve
9 g total fat; 7 g saturated fat; 881 mg sodium

Rich Fish Stew on Rosemary Mash

2 teaspoons olive oil

1 leek, chopped

1 clove garlic, crushed

1 teaspoon ground oregano

4 flat mushrooms, sliced

1 stalk celery, sliced

1 tablespoon no-added-salt tomato paste

2 zucchini (courgettes), sliced

400 g canned no-added-salt diced tomatoes

$^1/_2$ cup/125 mL dry white wine

500 g firm white fish fillets (e.g. gemfish, ling, barramundi, sea bass or blue-eye cod)

1 tablespoon chopped fresh basil

1 tablespoon chopped fresh parsley

ROSEMARY MASH

1 sprig fresh rosemary

2 teaspoons olive oil

2 large potatoes, chopped

$^1/_4$ cup/60 mL low-fat milk, warmed

ground white pepper

lemon juice, optional

1   **Rosemary mash:** Remove the leaves from the rosemary sprig. Place rosemary leaves and oil in a small saucepan over a low heat. Heat until warm. Remove pan from heat. Set aside to allow the flavours to develop – if possible do this several hours in advance, the longer the leaves can steep in the oil the more pronounced the flavour. Boil or microwave potatoes until tender. Drain well. Add milk and rosemary oil. Mash. Season with white pepper and lemon juice to taste. Keep warm or reheat just prior to serving.

2   Heat oil in a large deep-sided nonstick frying pan over a medium heat. Add leek and garlic. Cook, stirring, for 1-2 minutes or until soft. Add oregano, mushrooms and celery. Cook, stirring, for 2-3 minutes. Stir in tomato paste. Cook for 3-4 minutes or until it becomes deep red and develops a rich aroma.

3   Stir in zucchini, tomatoes and wine. Bring to the boil. Reduce heat. Simmer, stirring occasionally, for 5 minutes or until mixture starts to thicken.

4   Add fish. Cook for 6 minutes or until fish is just cooked – take care not to overcook or the fish will fall apart. Stir in basil and parsley.

5   To serve, place a mound of mash on each serving plate. Top with fish stew. Accompany with a green salad or steamed green vegetables of your choice.

Serves 4

1276 kilojoules/304 Calories – per serve
8 g total fat; 2 g saturated fat; 169 mg sodium

sweetfinishes

Stir-fried Fruit served with Lychee and Lemon Grass Ice Cream (page 138)

Stir-fried Fruit

1/4 cup/60 mL apple juice

**1 tablespoon finely grated fresh ginger
or finely chopped glacé ginger**

1 tablespoon palm or brown sugar or honey

**2-3 cups/370-550 g seasonal fresh fruit of your choice
(e.g. berries, pawpaw, pineapple, kiwi fruit, guava,
mango and banana)**

1/2 cup/125 mL white wine

1/4 cup/30 g slivered unsalted almonds, toasted

2 tablespoons shredded fresh mint

**1 quantity Lychee and Lemon Grass Ice Cream
(recipe follows)**

1   Place apple juice, ginger and sugar in a wok or nonstick frying pan over a medium heat. Cook, stirring, until sugar melts and sauce starts to thicken to a syrup.

2   Add fruit. Stir-fry for 1-2 minutes. Stir in wine. Cover and steam for 2-3 minutes. Scatter with almonds and mint.

3   Serve immediately with Lychee and Lemon Grass Ice Cream.
Serves 6

1177 kilojoules/284 Calories – per serve (with ice cream)
8 g total fat; 3 g saturated fat; 106 mg sodium
453 kilojoules/108 Calories – per serve (without ice cream)
3 g total fat; less than 1 g saturated fat; 10 mg sodium

Cook's tip: *For a creamy dish, use evaporated skim milk with a few drops coconut essence instead of the white wine.*

Lychee and Lemon Grass Ice Cream

2 stems fresh lemon grass, bruised and chopped

1/2 cup/125 mL evaporated skim milk

1/4 cup/60 mL apple juice

1 cup/185 g canned lychees, drained and juice reserved

1 tablespoon brown sugar

**500 g low-fat (less than 5% fat) vanilla ice cream,
softened**
1 quantity Stir-fried Fruit (recipe above)

1   Place lemon grass, milk and apple juice in a saucepan over a medium heat. Bring to the boil. Reduce heat. Simmer, stirring occasionally, for 10 minutes. Remove pan from heat. Steep for 1 hour or overnight – this allows the flavours to develop. Strain mixture. Discard lemon grass.

2   Preheat a grill to a high heat or oven to 220°C. Lightly spray or brush a baking tray with unsaturated oil.

3   Place lychees on baking tray. Sprinkle with sugar. Grill or bake until sugar melts and caramelises.

4   Reserve half of the lychees. Place the remainder in a food processor. Add milk and 2 tablespoons reserved lychee juice. Purée.

5   Dice remaining lychees. Stir diced lychees and purée into ice cream. Spoon into a freezerproof container. Freeze until solid. Serve with Stir-fried Fruit.
Serves 6

1177 kilojoules/284 Calories – per serve (with fruit)
8 g total fat; 3 g saturated fat; 106 mg sodium
723 kilojoules/175 Calories – per serve (without fruit)
5 g total fat; 3 g saturated fat; 96 mg sodium

Cook's tip: *It's best to make the ice cream a day or two before serving – this allows the flavours to develop fully. Or just make a large batch to have on hand as an easy healthy dessert.*

Whisky Bread and Peach Pudding

Whisky Bread and Peach Pudding

4 thick slices bread (try Italian, wholemeal or sourdough), cut into cubes – hand cut bread into 1.5-2 cm thick slices

1 cup/185 g diced peaches

$^1/_2$ cup/60 g sultanas or currants

2 tablespoons whisky or rum

2 eggs

2 cups/500 mL skim or low-fat milk

1 teaspoon vanilla essence

2 tablespoons brown sugar

1 teaspoon ground cinnamon

1   Preheat oven to 180°C. Lightly spray or brush a large ovenproof baking dish with unsaturated oil.

2   Place bread cubes, peaches and sultanas in baking dish. Toss to combine. Spread out evenly over base of dish. Sprinkle with whisky. Set aside.

3   Place eggs, milk, vanilla essence and 1 tablespoon sugar in a bowl. Whisk to combine. Pour over bread mixture. Combine cinnamon and remaining sugar. Sprinkle over top of pudding.

4   Bake for 35 minutes or until top is golden. If necessary, cover pudding and cook for 10 minutes longer or until set when tested with a knife.

Serves 6

669 kilojoules/160 Calories – per serve
2 g total fat; 1 g saturated fat; 120 mg sodium

Poached Ricotta Pears

4 pears, cored, peeled and halved

2 cups/500 mL red wine

1 cup/250 mL water

2 tablespoons sugar

1 cinnamon stick

PRUNE AND RICOTTA FILLING

¼ cup/55 g pitted prunes, halved

2 tablespoons port

¾ cup/185 g reduced-fat fresh ricotta cheese

½ teaspoon vanilla extract

1 teaspoon grated orange zest

1 tablespoon icing sugar

1   **Filling:** Place prunes and port in a saucepan. Bring to the boil. Remove pan from heat. Cool.

2   Place ricotta cheese, vanilla extract, orange zest and icing sugar in a food processor. Process until light and fluffy. Fold in prunes with 1-2 teaspoons of their liquid. Set aside.

3   Preheat oven to 180°C. Cut a sliver off the curved side of each pear so they sit flat. Place pears in a deep-sided frying pan, cavity side up.

4   Combine wine, water and sugar. Pour over pears to cover. Add cinnamon stick. Cover. Bring to simmering. Simmer for 10-15 minutes or until pears are just tender.

5   Using a slotted spoon, transfer pears to a baking dish. Spoon filling into cavities. Bake for 10 minutes or until filling is set.

6   Bring liquid remaining in frying pan to the boil. Boil until it reduces to a glaze consistency. Serve with pears.

Serves 4

1228 kilojoules/294 Calories – per serve
4 g total fat; 3 g saturated fat; 105 mg sodium

Cook's tip: *Heating the prunes in port adds a delicious flavour to this dish, but you could also use brandied prunes. If you don't like prunes, use any dried fruit of your choice or just the ricotta mixture.*

Layered Fruit Mould

1 cup/250 g low-fat vanilla frûche

½ cup/125 g reduced-fat fresh ricotta cheese

3 teaspoons gelatine

2 tablespoons hot water

85 g packet port wine or other jelly crystals of your choice

3 cups/750 g berries or fruit of choice except for fresh pineapple, kiwi fruit or pawpaw

1   Place frûche and ricotta cheese in a food processor. Process until smooth. Dissolve gelatine in hot water. Stir into frûche mixture.

2   Rinse eight 1 cup/250 mL capacity moulds or glasses with cold water. Divide frûche mixture between moulds. Chill until set.

3   Prepare jelly according to packet directions. Cool. Arrange fruit on top of set frûche mixture. Carefully pour over cooled jelly. Chill until set.

4   To serve, quickly dip moulds into a basin of hot water. Turn onto serving plates. Alternatively, serve straight from the glasses.

Serves 8

512 kilojoules/123 Calories – per serve
2 g total fat; 1 g saturated fat; 109 mg sodium

Cook's tip: *This dessert could be made in one large decorative mould, if you prefer.*
For an Italian touch, line individual dessert glasses with savoiardi sponge fingers, then top with the fruit. Pour over the jelly and when set, smooth over the frûche mixture.

Glazed Fruit in Hazelnut Filo Baskets

2 tablespoons roasted ground, unsalted hazelnuts or other unsalted nuts of your choice

1 teaspoon ground cinnamon

2 teaspoons sugar

6 sheets filo pastry

unsaturated oil or melted unsaturated margarine for brushing pastry

1/2 cup/120 g prepared blackcurrant jelly or flavour of your choice

3 cups/750 g chopped mixed fresh seasonal fruit (e.g. blueberries, pawpaw, kiwi fruit, peaches, raspberries, strawberries, mango, pineapple, passionfruit and melon)

icing sugar

CUSTARD CREAM

1/2 cup/125 mL low-fat custard

1/2 cup/125 g reduced-fat fresh ricotta cheese

1/4 cup/60 mL evaporated skim milk

1 teaspoon vanilla essence

1 **Custard cream:** Place custard, ricotta cheese, evaporated milk and vanilla essence in a blender. Process until smooth. Pour into a bowl. Cover. Refrigerate until ready to serve.

2 Preheat oven to 170°C. Lightly spray or brush four 1 cup/250 mL capacity ramekins with unsaturated oil. You can do this on the outside or inside of the ramekins, depending on whether you want to drape the pastry over the upturned 'mould' or lay it inside the dish as you would a pie. Be guided by the size and shape of the basket you want to end up with. Place dishes on a baking tray.

3 Place ground nuts, cinnamon and sugar in a small bowl. Mix to combine. Lay 2 sheets of filo pastry on a clean, dry surface. Lightly spray or brush with unsaturated oil. Sprinkle with half the nut mixture. Lay another 2 sheets of pastry on top. Repeat with oil and nut mixture. Top with remaining sheets of pastry. Cut the stack into quarters. Arrange pastry in or over dishes as described above. Bake for 10-15 minutes or until golden.

4 Just before serving, place jelly in a saucepan over a low heat. Melt. Add fruit. Toss to combine.

5 To serve, place a basket on each serving plate. Divide fruit mixture between baskets. Sprinkle with icing sugar and accompany with Custard Cream.

Makes 4 baskets

1407 kilojoules/340 Calories – per basket
10 g total fat; 3 g saturated fat; 300 mg sodium

Cook's tip: *The cooked and cooled baskets can be stored in an airtight container for up to 2 days.*

Macadamia and Coffee Marzipan

2 cups/270 g ground unsalted macadamias

2/3 cup/100 g pure icing sugar

1/2 cup/100 g caster sugar

6 teaspoons egg white (about 1 egg white)

1 tablespoon premium granulated coffee dissolved in 1 tablespoon of hot water or 1 teaspoon coffee essence

few drops vanilla essence

confectioner's rice paper

1 Place ground macadamias and icing and caster sugars in a food processor. Process to combine. With machine running, slowly add egg white. Process until mixture just holds together.

2 Divide mixture in half and place in two bowls. Add coffee to one portion. Knead to combine. Add vanilla essence to the other portion. Knead to combine.

3 Line an 18 cm square shallow cake tin with rice paper. Press the coffee-flavoured mixture firmly into the tin. Press vanilla-flavoured mixture on top. Cover lightly with greaseproof paper. Refrigerate overnight or until ready for use.

4 To serve, remove greaseproof paper. Cut into 3 cm squares or desired shapes.

Makes 36 pieces

295 kilojoules/72 Calories – per piece
6 g total fat; 1 g saturated fat; 1 mg sodium

Turkish Fig Sweets

3/4 cup/185 g tenderised or pre-soaked dried figs, roughly chopped

1/2 cup/70 g chopped dried apricots

1/2 cup/70 g pitted prunes, roughly chopped

2 tablespoons rose water or orange blossom water, plus additional for brushing

3/4 cup/100 g raw unsalted almonds or cashews, ground

1/4 cup/40 g pine nuts

2 sheets confectioner's rice paper

1   Place figs, apricots, prunes and rose water in a food processor. Process to combine. Add ground nuts. Process until mixture clumps into a ball.

2   Line an 18 cm shallow cake tin with a sheet of rice paper. Press fruit mixture evenly into tin. Scatter with pine nuts. Cover with remaining sheet of rice paper. Brush with a little more rose water. Chill until set.

3   Cut into small bars or desired shapes. Store in an airtight container in the refrigerator.

Makes 24 sweets

204 kilojoules/49 Calories – per sweet
3 g total fat; less than 1 g saturated fat; 2 mg sodium

Author's note: *These are an adaptation of a traditional Turkish sweet. They are very sweet, but have a subtle floral flavour that is delicious with coffee after a meal.*

Ingredients know-how: *Rose water, orange blossom water and rice paper are available from most health food stores, delicatessens and some supermarkets.*

Orange and Blueberry Upside-down Cakes

ORANGE AND BLUEBERRY TOPPING

2 small oranges, peeled

1 cup/155 g fresh or frozen blueberries

1 tablespoon cornflour

1 tablespoon brown sugar

2 tablespoons sherry or brandy

ALMOND CAKES

3/4 cup/115 g raw unsalted almonds, roasted and ground to a meal

3/4 cup/90 g plain flour

1 teaspoon baking powder

4 egg whites

1/2 cup/125 g sugar

2 egg yolks

1 teaspoon vanilla essence

ORANGE CUSTARD (OPTIONAL)

1 cup/250 mL low-fat custard

2 teaspoons orange blossom water, orange juice or orange-flavoured liqueur

2 teaspoons grated orange zest

1   **Custard:** Place custard, orange blossom water and orange zest in a jug. Mix to combine. Cover. Refrigerate until ready to use.

2   **Topping:** Place oranges in a saucepan. Pour over water to cover. Bring to the boil. Reduce heat. Simmer for 10 minutes. Drain. Set aside until cool enough to handle.

3   Preheat oven to 170°C. Lightly spray or brush two nonstick muffin trays with unsaturated oil.

4   Place blueberries, cornflour, sugar and sherry in a bowl. Toss to combine. Place an orange slice in the base of each muffin cup. Top with some of the blueberry mixture. Set aside.

5   **Cakes:** Sift together ground almonds, flour and baking powder. Place egg whites in a large bowl. Beat until soft peaks form. Gradually beat in sugar. Beat in egg yolks and vanilla essence. Continue beating until sugar dissolves.

6   Using a large spoon or spatula, fold in the flour mixture until just combined – take care not to overmix. Spoon batter into muffin cups. Bake for 15-20 minutes or until cooked when tested with a skewer. Stand muffins in tins for 5-10 minutes. Turn onto a wire rack. Serve warm with Orange Custard, if desired.

Makes 12 cakes

748 kilojoules/181 Calories – per cake (with custard)
6 g total fat; 1 g saturated fat; 65 mg sodium
669 kilojoules/162 Calories – per cake (without custard)
6 g total fat; 1 g saturated fat; 48 mg sodium

Apricot Risotto (page 146)

Turkish Fig Sweets

*Orange and Blueberry
Upside-down Cakes*

Sweet Potato Tart

½ **quantity Sweet Almond Pastry (page 169)**

SWEET POTATO FILLING

400 g red sweet potato (kumera), scrubbed

¼ cup/60 mL maple syrup

1 egg

3 egg whites

**½ cup/100 g low-fat fruit yogurt of your choice
(peach, apricot or passionfruit are all delicious choices)**

1 teaspoon ground ginger

1 teaspoon ground cinnamon

½ teaspoon ground nutmeg

½ teaspoon ground allspice

1   Preheat oven to 180°C. Lightly spray or brush a 23 cm pie dish with unsaturated oil.

2   Roll out pastry. Line the pie dish. Crimp edges and prick base a few times with a fork. Cover with plastic food wrap. Chill until ready to use.

3   **Filling:** Roast sweet potato in its skin for 40 minutes or until soft. Peel. Press flesh through a sieve to remove any hard fibrous pieces. There should be a good 1½ cups/350 g of flesh.

4   Place sweet potato, maple syrup, egg, egg whites, yogurt, ginger, cinnamon, nutmeg and allspice in a food processor. Purée. Pour mixture into prepared pastry case. Bake for 40 minutes or until set – a knife inserted in the centre should come out clean.
Makes a 23 cm round pie – cuts into 12 slices

706 kilojoules/171 Calories – per slice
6 g total fat; 1 g saturated fat; 70 mg sodium

Apricot Risotto

2½ cups/600 mL low-fat milk

1 tablespoon sugar

1 vanilla bean or 1 teaspoon vanilla essence or almond-flavoured liqueur

2 teaspoons unsaturated margarine

½ cup/90 g diced dried apricots

¾ cup/140 g arborio or calrose rice

1 cup/250 mL sparkling apple juice or cider

6 tablespoons puréed fresh or canned apricots

2 tablespoons flaked unsalted almonds, toasted

1   Place milk, sugar and vanilla bean in a saucepan over a medium heat. Bring to simmering. Reduce heat to very low – take care not to allow the milk to boil.

2   Melt margarine in a separate large saucepan over a low heat. Add apricots. Cook, stirring, for 1-2 minutes. Increase heat to medium. Add rice. Cook, stirring, for 1-2 minutes longer. Add apple juice. Cook, stirring frequently, until liquid is absorbed. Add ¾ cup/185 mL of the hot milk and cook as described above. Continue adding milk, ¾ cup/185 mL at a time until all the milk is used and the rice is tender – it will take 20-25 minutes to add all the milk.

3   To serve, stir apricot purée into rice. Spoon into warm bowls. Scatter with almonds.
Serves 6

971 kilojoules/235 Calories – per serve
9 g total fat; 1 g saturated fat; 68 mg sodium

Cook's tip: *If you don't want to be cooking this while the main course is being eaten, cook in advance and keep warm, or reheat in a low oven. You may need to add a little more milk to bring the risotto back to its original creamy texture.*
Try this dessert with apricots, pears, apples, strawberries or other fruit with your favourite matching liqueur. Or, for an Asian version, try sautéing ginger with Thai sticky rice. Use evaporated skim milk with a few drops of coconut essence as the liquid and mango, kiwi fruit or star fruit as the fruit.

Peach Amaretto Crumble

6 amaretti biscuits

2 tablespoons unsalted almonds, roughly chopped or ground

1 tablespoon brown sugar

2 teaspoons almond-flavoured liqueur or orange blossom water

2 large canned peaches in natural juice or fresh peaches, peeled

2 tablespoons juice from canned peaches or orange juice

1   Preheat oven to 175°C. Lightly spray or brush a small baking dish or two ramekins with unsaturated oil.

2   Place biscuits, almonds and sugar in a food processor. Process to make a crumble. Add liqueur. Using the pulse button, process to incorporate.

3   Cut peaches in slices. Place in the base of the baking dish or ramekins. Pour over peach juice. Scatter with crumble mixture. If desired, sprinkle with a little extra liqueur.

4   Bake for 15-20 minutes or until topping is golden and peaches are tender. Serve with thick low-fat natural yogurt or frûche.
Serves 2

1470 kilojoules/356 Calories – per serve
18 g total fat; 3 g saturated fat; 127 mg sodium

Frozen Mango Blush

2 large mangos, diced and frozen – about 2 cups/370 g mango flesh

4 strawberries

1¼ cups/250 g low-fat yogurt of choice – natural, passionfruit or apricot all work well for this dessert

1-2 tablespoons orange juice or sparkling wine

Allow mangos to soften slightly (so you don't ruin the blades of your food processor), then place in a food processor. Add strawberries and yogurt. Using the pulse button, process to combine. With motor running, slowly add orange juice. Process until desired consistency is achieved. Serve immediately or freeze and serve as a refreshing summer ice.
Serves 4

457 kilojoules/110 Calories – per serve
less than 1 g total fat; less than 1 g saturated fat; 41 mg sodium

Author's note: *Depending on how much liquid you add, this recipe can be both a refreshing summer drink or an elegant frozen dessert. Be careful not to add too much at first as it will lose body quickly. Experiment with other fruits and combinations of your choice.*

Macadamia and Coffee Marzipan
(page 142)

Mixed Berry and Ricotta Lasagne
(page 150)

Peach Amaretto Crumble

Mixed Berry and Ricotta Lasagne

2 cups/500 g reduced-fat fresh ricotta cheese

icing sugar

2 teaspoons vanilla essence, or berry- or orange-flavoured liqueur

6 thick lasagne sheets

2 cups/310 g fresh seasonal or thawed frozen mixed berries (e.g. blueberries, raspberries, blackberries or strawberries or any other fruit of your choice)

2 tablespoons chopped unsalted walnuts, optional

1   Place ricotta cheese, 1 tablespoon icing sugar and vanilla essence in a bowl. Beat with an electric mixer until light and fluffy. Alternatively, whip in a food processor. Cover. Chill until ready to use.

2   Bring a large saucepan of water to the boil. Add lasagne sheets. Cook, stirring occasionaly, until *al dente*. Drain well.

3   Cut each sheet of lasagne in half. Place on a warm baking tray lined with nonstick baking paper. If you are not going to assemble the lasagne immediately, cover with a damp clean cloth to prevent drying out. Just prior to assembly, sprinkle with a little water and warm in the oven or microwave to ensure that the dough is still soft and supple.

4   To assemble, place one square of lasagne on each warm serving plate. Sprinkle lightly with icing sugar. Spread with ricotta cheese mixture. Scatter with berries. Top with another lasagne sheet. Spread with remaining ricotta cheese mixture. Sprinkle top of each stack with walnuts and icing sugar. Serve immediately.

Serves 4

1050 kilojoules/253 Calories – per serve (with walnuts)
16 g total fat; 7 g saturated fat; 235 mg sodium
837 kilojoules/201 Calories – per serve (without walnuts)
11 g total fat; 7 g saturated fat; 234 mg sodium

Cook's tip: *Fresh ricotta cheese is available from delicatessens and should be used for this recipe. It has a smoother texture than that which is available in tubs from supermarkets and is a better choice when you want a mixture to be smooth.*

Frozen Mango Blush (page 148)

home**bakes**

Pumpkin and Banana Loaf

1 cup/125 g self-raising flour

1/2 cup/75 g wholemeal self-raising flour

1/4 teaspoon bicarbonate of soda

1 teaspoon ground ginger

1 teaspoon ground nutmeg

1 teaspoon ground cinnamon

1/4 teaspoon ground allspice

1/2 cup/90 g brown sugar

100 mL olive oil

1/4 cup/60 mL buttermilk or low-fat natural yogurt

2 eggs

2 cups/250 g grated pumpkin

1 ripe banana, mashed

1/2 cup/60 g sultanas

1/3 cup/40 g chopped unsalted walnuts or pecans

1 quantity Candied Orange Frosting (page 164), optional

icing sugar, optional

1 Preheat oven to 180°C. Lightly spray or brush a 14 x 22 cm loaf tin with unsaturated oil and dust with flour, or line with nonstick baking paper.

2 Sift together flours, bicarbonate of soda, ginger, nutmeg, cinnamon and allspice into a large bowl. Add sugar. Place oil, buttermilk and eggs in a separate bowl. Whisk to combine. Pour into flour mixture. Beat with an electric mixer for 1 minute.

3 Stir in pumpkin, banana, sultanas and walnuts. Mix to combine. Pour batter into prepared tin. Bake for 1 hour or until cooked when tested with a skewer. Stand in tin for 5-10 minutes. Turn loaf onto a wire rack to cool. Spread cold loaf with Candied Orange Frosting or sprinkle with icing sugar.

Makes a 14 x 22 cm loaf – cuts into 20 slices

695 kilojoules/168 Calories – per slice (with frosting)
7 g total fat; 1 g saturated fat; 87 mg sodium
547 kilojoules/132 Calories – per slice (without frosting)
7 g total fat; 1 g saturated fat; 86 mg sodium

Fresh Ginger, Orange and Almond Cake

5-6 cm/50-60 g nob fresh ginger, peeled

1 large orange

3/4 cup/185 g sugar, plus 1/4 cup/60 g extra

3/4 cup/185 mL buttermilk

1 teaspoon vanilla essence

2 egg yolks

1 3/4 cups/215 g plain flour

1 teaspoon baking powder

1/2 teaspoon bicarbonate of soda

1 1/2 cups/140 g almond meal

2 tablespoons diced preserved ginger

4 egg whites

fresh orange slices, optional

icing sugar

1 Preheat oven to 175°C. Lightly spray or brush a 28 cm round cake tin with unsaturated oil and dust with flour, or line with nonstick baking paper.

2 Place ginger in a small saucepan. Pour over water to cover. Bring to the boil. Boil for 10 minutes. Cool. Grate coarsely. Place in a food processor.

3 Scrub orange. Cut into 8 segments. Remove seeds and thick white pieces of pith. Add orange segments, the 3/4 cup/185 g of sugar, milk, vanilla essence and egg yolks to the food processor. Process until smooth.

4 Sift together flour, baking powder and bicarbonate of soda into a large bowl. Add almond meal, preserved ginger and orange mixture. Mix to combine.

5 Place egg whites in a separate bowl. Beat until soft peaks form. Gradually beat in remaining 1/4 cup/60 g of sugar. Continue beating until sugar dissolves. Fold egg white mixture into orange mixture. Pour into prepared tin.

6 Bake for 1 hour or until golden and cooked when tested with a skewer. Stand tin on a wire rack for 10 minutes. Turn cake onto wire rack to cool. Decorate with fresh orange slices and sprinkle with icing sugar, if desired. Alternatively, simply sprinkle with icing sugar.

Makes a 28 cm cake – cuts into 20 slices

495 kilojoules/120 Calories – per slice
5 g total fat; less than 1 g saturated fat; 51 mg sodium

Pumpkin and Banana Loaf topped with Candied Orange Frosting

Pistachio and Almond Amaretti

3/4 cup/110 g unsalted pistachios, ground

3/4 cup/140 g almond meal

1/2 cup/60 g self-raising flour

2 egg whites

1/2 cup/100 g caster sugar

1 teaspoon honey

1 teaspoon grated orange zest

1   Preheat oven to 150°C. Line two baking trays with nonstick baking paper.

2   Sift together ground pistachios, almond meal and flour into a bowl. Place egg whites in a separate large bowl. Beat until soft peaks form. Gradually beat in sugar and honey. Continue beating, until sugar dissolves. Stir in flour mixture and orange zest.

3   Place teaspoons of mixture on prepared baking trays. Bake for 15 minutes or until pale golden. Transfer to wire racks to cool.
Makes 24 biscuits

766 kilojoules/186 Calories – per biscuit
9 g total fat; 1 g saturated fat; 101 mg sodium

Author's note: *This recipe is an adaptation of the traditional Italian amaretti which you often find accompanying coffee in Italian cafes. Normally flour is not used, however, I prefer the texture and it also brings down the fat content quite a bit (even though the fat in nuts is good fat). Try using other nuts such as hazelnuts, walnuts or even pine nuts for a change. Hazelnut Amaretti made with hazelnuts instead of pistachios and coffee essence instead of orange zest is a deliciously rich treat.*

Spiced Pear Cake

3/4 cup/170 g caster sugar

80 g unsaturated margarine, melted

1 egg

2/3 cup/170 mL buttermilk

2/3 cup/125 g chopped canned pears in natural juice or 1 cup/135 g grated fresh pear

3 tablespoons juice from the canned pears or apple juice if using fresh pear

1/2 teaspoon almond essence

2 cups/250 g self-raising flour

1/2 cup/60 g semolina

1 teaspoon freshly ground black pepper

1 teaspoon ground cardamom

1 teaspoon ground mixed spice

1 quantity Lemon Yogurt Icing (page 177), optional

icing sugar, optional

1   Preheat oven to 180°C. Lightly spray or brush a 22 cm kugelhof cake tin with unsaturated oil. Dust with flour or semolina.

2   Place sugar in a small bowl. Pour over melted margarine. Mix to combine. Transfer to a food processor. Add egg, buttermilk, pears, juice and almond essence. Process until smooth and light.

3   Sift together flour, semolina, black pepper, cardamom and mixed spice into a large bowl. Make a well in the centre of the dry ingredients. Add liquid mixture. Mix lightly to combine.

4   Pour batter into prepared tin. Bake for 1 hour 15 minutes or until cooked when tested with a skewer. Stand tin on a wire rack for 5-10 minutes. Turn cake onto wire rack to cool.

5   To serve, drizzle with Lemon Yogurt Icing or simply dust with icing sugar.
Makes a 22 cm kugelhof or ring cake – cuts into 20 slices

591 kilojoules/144 Calories – per slice (with icing)
4 g total fat; 1 g saturated fat; 127 mg sodium
527 kilojoules/128 Calories – per slice (without icing)
4 g total fat; 1 g saturated fat; 126 mg sodium

Author's note: *This cake is hard to resist, served straight out of the oven when it's piping hot with a crunchy crust. You could use apples instead of pears if you wish.*

Dried Fruit Sandwiches

GINGER AND FRUIT FILLING

1/2 cup/110 g pitted prunes, chopped

1/2 cup/75 g currants

1/4 cup/30 g raisins

2 tablespoons glacé ginger, diced

1/2 cup/125 mL water

1/4 cup/25 g unsalted pecans, chopped

1 tablespoon brown sugar

1 tablespoon grated orange zest

1 tablespoon orange juice

BISCUITS

1/2 cup/125 g sugar

2 tablespoons unsaturated margarine

1/4 cup/60 mL unsaturated oil

1 egg, beaten

few drops almond essence

2 cups/250 g plain flour

1 teaspoon baking powder

1 **Filling:** Place prunes, currants, raisins, ginger and water in a saucepan over a low heat. Bring to simmering. Simmer until liquid is absorbed. Cool slightly. Transfer to a food processor. Add pecans, brown sugar and orange zest and juice. Process to make a coarse paste. Cool.

2 **Biscuits:** Using an electric mixer or a blender, cream sugar, margarine and oil until light and fluffy. Gradually beat in egg and almond essence. Continue beating until mixture is smooth. Sift together flour and baking powder. Fold into mixture. Shape mixture into a ball. Wrap in plastic food wrap. Chill for 30 minutes or overnight.

3 Preheat oven to180°C. Line two baking trays with nonstick baking paper.

4 Place dough between sheets of nonstick baking paper or plastic food wrap. Roll out to form a 3-4 mm thick rectangle. Cut into 4 cm squares. Place half the squares on the prepared baking trays. Place a spoonful of filling in the centre. Cover with remaining dough squares. Press edges to seal. Bake for 12-15 minutes or until golden. Cool on wire racks.

Makes 20 biscuits

620 kilojoules/150 Calories – per biscuit
6 g total fat; 1 g saturated fat; 22 mg sodium

Coffee and Ginger Almond Bread

1 cup/125 g plain flour

2 teaspoons good quality ground coffee

3 egg whites

1/2 cup/100 g caster sugar

3/4 cup/105 g unsalted almonds or hazelnuts

1/2 cup/110 g finely diced glacé ginger

1 Preheat oven to 170°C. Lightly spray or brush a 7 x 24 cm bar tin with unsaturated oil.

2 Sift together flour and coffee into a bowl. Place egg whites in a separate bowl. Beat until soft peaks form. Gradually beat in sugar. Continue beating until sugar dissolves. Fold in flour mixture. Fold in nuts and ginger.

3 Spoon batter into prepared tin. Bake for 35 minutes. Stand tin on a wire rack. Cool completely. When cold, remove bread from tin. Wrap in aluminium foil. Store in a cool place for 1-3 days – the finished bread will be crisper if you can leave it for 2-3 days.

4 Preheat oven to 120°C. Using a very sharp serrated or electric knife, cut cooked loaf into wafer thin slices. Place slices on ungreased baking trays. Bake for 45-60 minutes or until dry and crisp. Cool on wire racks. Store in an airtight container.

Makes 40 pieces

157 kilojoules/38 Calories – per piece
1 g total fat; less than 1 g saturated fat; 4 mg sodium

Author's note: *This recipe is only limited by your imagination. You could use any nut, dried fruit or spice you fancy. For something festive, try cherries, mixed peel and brazil nuts, or for an exotic eastern feel use pistachios, glacé pears and ground cardamom.*

Caribbean Fruit Cake (page 160)

Coffee and Ginger Almond Bread

Dried Fruit Sandwiches

Caribbean Fruit Cake

1 cup/250 mL water

1/2 cup/90 g brown sugar

1 1/2 cups/280 g mixed dried fruit

1/2 cup/125 mL canned crushed pineapple

2 tablespoons unsaturated margarine

2 tablespoons port

1 teaspoon ground cinnamon

1/2 teaspoon ground nutmeg

1/2 teaspoon ground mixed spice

1 tablespoon coffee and chicory essence or 2 teaspoons granulated coffee dissolved in 1 tablespoon water, optional

2 cups/250 g plain flour

1 1/4 cups/200 g wholemeal flour

1/4 cup/25 g wheatgerm

2 teaspoons baking powder

1 teaspoon bicarbonate of soda

1 tablespoon warm water

unsalted flaked almonds

1   Preheat oven to 180°C. Lightly spray or brush a 23 cm square cake tin with unsaturated oil, then line with nonstick baking paper.

2   Place water, sugar, mixed fruit, pineapple, margarine, port, cinnamon, nutmeg, mixed spice and coffee essence in a large saucepan over a medium heat. Bring to the boil. Remove pan from heat. Set aside until warm.

3   Sift together flours, wheatgerm and baking powder. Dissolve bicarbonate of soda in the warm water. Stir into flour mixture. Add warm fruit mixture to flour mixture. Mix to combine.

4   Pour into prepared tin. Level top. Scatter with almonds. Bake for 30-35 minutes or until cooked when tested with a skewer. Stand in tin for 5 minutes. Turn cake onto a wire rack covered with a piece of nonstick paper – so you don't lose the almonds. Turn back onto another wire rack. Cool. Serve warm or cold.

Makes a 23 cm square cake – cuts into 16 squares

802 kilojoules/193 Calories – per square
3 g total fat; less than 1 g saturated fat; 117 mg sodium

Author's note: *This recipe has evolved over many 'cookings' from one of my favourite recipes of Graham Kerr's – a great inspiration and friend. I've never met anyone with so many 'tricks' to make low-fat food taste and feel like you're eating the real thing. In this cake, his tricks include adding the spices and fruit to cold water to allow the flavours to infuse, and mixing the bicarbonate of soda with water apparently helps an eggless cake rise without the metallic after-taste.*

Rosemary, Lemon and Pine Nut Bread

2 tablespoons grated lemon zest

2 tablespoons fresh rosemary or 1 tablespoon dried rosemary

2 tablespoons pine nuts

2 cups/250 g self-raising flour

1 cup/155 g grated parsnip or potato

1 tablespoon grated parmesan cheese

1 cup/250 mL buttermilk

1 tablespoon extra virgin olive oil, optional

2 tablespoons lemon juice

1 tablespoon plain flour

1   Preheat oven to 190°C. Lightly brush or spray a 14 x 22 cm loaf tin with unsaturated oil and dust with flour.

2   Place lemon zest, rosemary and pine nuts in a bowl. Mix to combine. Combine flour, parsnip and parmesan cheese in a separate bowl. Make a well in the centre of the flour mixture. Beat together buttermilk, oil and lemon juice. Pour into well in flour mixture. Mix quickly and lightly to form a soft dough.

3   Press half the mixture into prepared tin. Scatter with half the pine nut mixture. Top with remaining mixture. Mix remaining pine nut mixture with the plain flour. Sprinkle over surface of loaf. Bake for 40-45 minutes or until golden and loaf sounds hollow when tapped with your knuckles.

Makes a 14 x 22 cm loaf – cuts into 20 slices

318 kilojoules/77 Calories – per slice
3 g total fat; less than 1 g saturated fat; 102 mg sodium

Pecan Date Brownies

1 cup/185 g pitted seeded dates

1/2 cup/60 g chopped unsalted pecans

1 cup/125 g self-raising flour

1/2 teaspoon bicarbonate of soda

1/3 cup/40 g cocoa powder

1/2 cup/125 mL apple sauce or canned pie apple

1/2 cup/125 mL buttermilk or low-fat milk

1 teaspoon vanilla essence

4 egg whites

1/4 cup/45 g brown sugar

1   Preheat oven to 190°C. Lightly spray or brush a 21 x 28 cm shallow cake tin with unsaturated oil and line with nonstick baking paper. Alternatively, you can use a 23 cm square cake tin.

2   Place dates in a bowl. Pour over boiling water to cover. Soak for 20 minutes. Drain. Press to remove excess moisture. Place half the dates in a separate bowl. Add pecans. Mix to combine. Set aside. Sift together flour, bicarbonate of soda and cocoa powder into a separate bowl. Set aside.

3   Place remaining dates in a food processor. Add apple sauce, milk and vanilla essence. Process until smooth. Place egg whites in a large bowl. Beat until soft peaks form. Gradually beat in sugar. Continue beating until sugar dissolves.

4   Fold egg whites into apple mixture. Fold in cocoa mixture. Mix until just combined – take care not to overmix. Spoon batter into prepared tin. Scatter with dates and pecan mixture, pressing slightly into surface. Bake for 20-25 minutes or until cooked when tested with a skewer. Stand in tin for 10 minutes. Turn brownies onto a wire rack to cool. Cut into squares. Store in an airtight container.

Makes 24 squares

313 kilojoules/75 Calories – per square
2 g total fat; less than 1 g saturated fat; 73 mg sodium

Cherry and Walnut Teacake

1/4 cup/45 g brown sugar

3/4 cup/185 mL buttermilk

1/2 cup/125 mL skim milk

1 egg

2 tablespoons unsaturated oil

2 cups/250 g self-raising flour

1/3 cup/30 g wheatgerm

1 1/2 cups/300 g canned pitted cherries, well drained, or you might like to try blueberries or raspberries

CRUNCHY WALNUT TOPPING

1/4 cup/30 g crushed unsalted walnuts

2 tablespoons sugar

1 teaspoon ground cinnamon

1   Preheat oven to 190°C. Lightly spray or brush a 20 cm square cake tin with unsaturated oil.

2   **Topping:** Place walnuts, sugar and cinnamon in a small bowl. Mix to combine. Set aside.

3   Place sugar, buttermilk, milk, egg and oil in a bowl. Whisk to combine. Sift together flour and wheatgerm. Mix into milk mixture until just combined – do not overmix. Fold in cherries.

4   Spoon mixture into prepared tin. Sprinkle with topping. Bake for 30 minutes or until golden and cooked when tested with a skewer. Stand in tin for 5 minutes. Turn cake onto a wire rack. Serve warm or cold.

Makes a 20 cm square cake – cuts into 16 squares

551 kilojoules/134 Calories – per square
5 g total fat; 1 g saturated fat; 124 mg sodium

Ingredient know-how: *Wheat germ is the heart of the wheat grain and has a high oil and vitamin E content. It adds a delicious nutty flavour to baked goods, and helps make a 'short' texture in pastries and cakes that are lower in fat. It can become rancid over time, so store in the refrigerator or freezer and buy in smaller quantities that will be used within the use-by time.*

Cherry and Walnut Teacake

Pecan Date Brownies

Currant Buttermilk Scones

2 cups/250 g self-raising flour

¹⁄₂ cup/75 g currants

2 teaspoons mixed peel

1 cup/250 mL buttermilk

1 tablespoon unsaturated oil

low-fat milk

1 quantity Orange Blossom Cream (recipe follows), optional

marmalade, optional

1   Preheat oven to 210°C. Lightly spray or brush a baking tray with unsaturated oil or line with nonstick baking paper.

2   Sift flour into a large bowl. Add currants and mixed peel. Mix to combine. Make a well in the centre of the dry ingredients. Place buttermilk and oil in a bowl. Whisk to combine. Pour into well in dry ingredients. Mix quickly and lightly with a round bladed knife to make a soft dough.

3   Turn dough onto a floured board. Knead gently until smooth. Press or roll into a 2 cm thick rectangle. Using a 3 cm scone cutter, cut out scones. Place on prepared baking tray. Bake for 8-10 minutes or until golden. Serve with Orange Blossom Cream and marmalade, if desired.

Makes 10 scones

564 kilojoules/136 Calories – per scone (plain)
3 g total fat; less than 1 g saturated fat; 191 mg sodium
675 kilojoules/163 Calories – per scone (with Orange Blossom Cream and marmalade)
4 g total fat; 2 g saturated fat; 230 mg sodium

Orange Blossom Cream

1 cup/250 g reduced-fat fresh ricotta cheese

2 teaspoons orange blossom water

1 teaspoon grated orange zest

Place ricotta cheese, orange blossom water and orange zest in a bowl or food processor. Beat or process until light and fluffy.

Makes 1 cup/250 mL

112 kilojoules/27 Calories – per 1 tablespoon
2 g total fat; 1 g saturated fat; 39 mg sodium

Candied Orange Frosting

¹⁄₂ small orange, thinly sliced

1 tablespoon sugar

1 cup/155 g icing sugar

1 tablespoon low-fat natural yogurt

Place orange and sugar in a saucepan over a low heat. Cook until orange is soft and mixture is syrupy. Cool slightly. Place in a food processor. Add icing sugar and yogurt. Using the pulse button, process until mixture is combined.

2967 kilojoules/715 Calories – analysis for total quantity
less than 1 g total fat; nil saturated fat; 16 mg sodium

Currant Buttermilk Scones served with Orange Blossom Cream and marmalade

thebasics

pastries

Ricotta Pastry

2 cups/250 g self-raising flour

¹/₂ cup/125 g low-fat ricotta cheese

¹/₂ cup/125 mL buttermilk

1 egg white

2 tablespoons unsaturated oil

1-2 tablespoons chilled skim milk

1   Place flour, ricotta cheese, buttermilk, egg white and oil in food processor. Using the pulse button, process until just combined.

2   With machine running, slowly add skim milk until mixture forms a dough.

3   Turn pastry onto a lightly floured surface. Knead into a ball. Wrap pastry in plastic food wrap. Refrigerate for at least 30 minutes or until ready to use.
Makes enough to cover a 20 cm round pie

6022 kilojoules/1457 Calories – analysis for total quantity
56 g total fat; 14 g saturated fat; 2113 mg sodium

Author's note: *This pastry is suitable for all savoury pies, quiches, pasties or recipes that call for shortcrust pastry. You can also use it instead of puff pastry. It won't form the flakes or be as puffy, but it will taste as good. Recipes in this book which use this pastry are Middle Eastern Chicken Pasties (page 130) and Steak and Oyster Pot Pie (page 124).*

Polenta Pastry

1 cup/125 g self-raising flour

³/₄ cup/125 g polenta (cornmeal)

2 tablespoons olive oil

³/₄ cup/185 mL buttermilk or use a mixture of half low-fat natural yogurt and half low-fat milk

1   Sift together flour and polenta into a bowl. Make a well in the centre. Place milk and oil in a jug. Mix to combine. Pour into well in centre of flour mixture. Mix to make a soft dough.

2   Turn onto a lightly floured surface. Knead until smooth. Wrap in plastic food wrap. Refrigerate until ready to use.
Makes enough to cover a 20 cm round pie

6050 kilojoules/1468 Calories – analysis for total quantity
48 g total fat; 9 g saturated fat; 1288 mg sodium

Author's note: *This light, crusty pastry can be used for any savoury pie. In this book, I have used it for the Chilli Turkey Pot Pie (page 112). For added colour and flavour, sprinkle with paprika or add seasonings such as chilli, fresh herbs or finely chopped pimento to the dough.*

Sweet Almond Pastry

1 cup/125 g flour

¹/₂ cup/60 g self-raising flour

¹/₂ cup/55 g ground almonds

1 tablespoon wheatgerm

1 tablespoon cornflour

1 tablespoon sugar

1¹/₂ tablespoons unsaturated margarine

100 mL chilled skim milk

50 mL cold water, optional

1   Place flours, almonds, wheatgerm, cornflour and sugar in a food processor. Using the pulse button, process until just combined.

2   Add margarine. Using the pulse button, process until mixture resembles fine breadcrumbs.

3   With machine running, slowly add milk until mixture forms a ball. If necessary add water.

4   Turn pastry onto a lightly floured surface. Knead briefly, until pastry is smooth. Wrap in plastic food wrap. Refrigerate for at least 30 minutes or until ready to use.
Makes enough to line a 23 cm round pie plate

5896 kilojoules/1431 Calories – analysis for total quantity
64 g total fat; 8 g saturated fat; 469 mg sodium

Cook's tip: *Use this pastry for any sweet pies, tarts or recipes that call for sweet shortcrust pastry.*

ways with vegetables

ROASTED PEPPERS
Roasting peppers, particularly red peppers, gives them a rich and flavoursome character. Roasted peppers can be sliced and tossed through salads or pasta, puréed for sauces and dips or tossed with a simple dressing such the Traditional Balsamic Dressing (page 173) and used on an antipasto platter.

To roast peppers: Preheat grill to very hot or oven to 220°C. Cut peppers in half, lengthwise. Remove seeds. Gently flatten with your hands. Place peppers skin side up under grill or place on a baking tray. Grill or bake until skins blister and blacken. Place peppers in a paper or plastic food bag. Stand for 10 minutes or until cool enough to handle. Remove skins. Use as required.

GRILLED EGGPLANT AND ZUCCHINI
In Mediterranean cooking, eggplant (aubergine) and, to a lesser extent, zucchini (courgettes), are used widely as a flavouring, a base for dips and in pasta sauces. They are commonly sliced, layered in a colander and sprinkled with salt, then left to drain for 30 minutes. This removes any bitter juices and softens the vegetable. Before using, they are rinsed well under cold running water to remove most of the salt. If you prefer to avoid salt, place the eggplant or zucchini slices in a microwavable dish. Cover. Cook on HIGH (100%) for 30-60 seconds or until vegetables just start to soften.

To grill or barbecue eggplant and zucchini: Preheat grill or barbecue to hot. Prepare as described above. Pat dry on absorbent kitchen paper. Place vegetables under grill or on lightly oiled barbecue grill. Cook for 5 minutes each side or until vegetables are soft and golden.

To roast eggplant for using in dips: Preheat oven to 200°C. Leave the eggplant whole. Using a skewer or fork, pierce the skin several times. Place in a roasting dish. Bake for 25-30 minutes or until flesh is very soft. Remove skin. Purée or mash flesh with flavourings such as lemon juice, crushed garlic, tahini, chopped fresh herbs, freshly ground black pepper and olive oil. Use as a dip or spread.

CARAMELISED ONIONS
Caramelised onions are great for adding a rich flavour and texture to low-fat dishes. Use on pizzas, in frittatas, tossed through pasta or served with grilled meat or chicken.

To caramelise onions: Peel red, brown or white onions. Slice. Heat a little unsaturated oil in a large nonstick frying pan over a medium heat. Add onions. Reduce heat to medium-low. Cook, stirring frequently, for 20-30 minutes or until onions are soft and golden. For extra flavouring, stir in a good quality red or white wine or balsamic vinegar and/or chopped fresh herbs at the end of cooking.

sauces and dressings

Roasted Chilli Tomato Salsa

1 cup/60 g diced plum tomatoes

1/2 cup/60 g finely chopped green onions

1 teaspoon finely chopped fresh red chilli

2 teaspoons lime juice

1 teaspoon chilli sauce

1 teaspoon olive oil

1   Preheat oven to 170°C. Lightly spray or brush a baking dish with unsaturated oil.

2   Combine tomatoes, green onions, chilli, lime juice, chilli sauce and oil in prepared baking dish. Bake for 15 minutes or until onions are soft and mixture aromatic. Serve warm or cold.
Makes 1 cup/250 mL

19 kilojoules/4 Calories – per 2 tablespoons
less than 1 g total fat; nil saturated fat; 11 mg sodium

Cook's tip: *This salsa is delicious served with grilled meat or chicken or Mexican-style dishes such as the White Bean Nachos (page 38). For an extra flavour boost, try tossing it through pasta or adding to casseroles or meatloaves.*

Fresh Caribbean Tomato Salsa

2 plum tomatoes, diced

2 tablespoons diced cucumber or green pepper

2 tablespoons diced fresh pineapple

1 tablespoon diced red onion or shallots

1 tablespoon chopped fresh coriander or mint

2 tablespoons lime juice

1 tablespoon white wine vinegar

freshly ground black pepper

Place tomatoes, cucumber, pineapple, onion, coriander, lime juice, vinegar and black pepper to taste in a glass or ceramic bowl. Toss to combine. Cover. Store in the refrigerator until ready to use. Best used within a few hours of making.
Makes 2 cups/500 mL

22 kilojoules/5 Calories – per 2 tablespoons
nil total fat; nil saturated fat; 2 mg sodium

Cook's tip: *Try this salsa with grilled salmon, swordfish or chicken. It is also delicious served with Louisiana-crusted Chicken (page 120), spooned on bruschetta or tossed through hot barbecued prawns.*

Mango and Coriander Salsa

1 mango or pawpaw, diced

1/2 small Lebanese cucumber, diced

1/2 small red onion, diced

4 tablespoons finely chopped fresh coriander

juice of 1 lime

1 tablespoon low-fat natural yogurt

Place mango, cucumber, onion, coriander, lime juice and yogurt in a bowl. Mix to combine. Cover. Refrigerate until ready to use. Best used within a few hours of making.
Makes 1 1/2 cups/375 mL

16 kilojoules/4 Calories – per 2 tablespoons
nil total fat; nil saturated fat; 1 mg sodium

Cook's tip: *Try this tropical salsa with simply cooked poultry or fish. Peaches are a great alternative to the mango or pawpaw.*

Salsa Verde

1 cup/30 g fresh basil leaves

1/2 cup/15 g fresh parsley sprigs

1/2 cup/15 g fresh mint leaves

1 tablespoon capers, rinsed and drained

2 tablespoons red wine vinegar

1 tablespoon lemon juice

2 teaspoons olive oil

Place basil, parsley, mint, capers, vinegar, lemon juice and oil in a blender or food processor. Using the pulse button, process to make a coarse purée. Transfer to bowl. Cover. Store in the refrigerator for up to 3 days.

Makes 1/2 cup/125 mL

73 kilojoules/18 Calories – per 1 tablespoon
2 g total fat; less than 1 g saturated fat; 50 mg sodium

Cook's tip: *Use this sauce to dress up grilled or simply cooked fish, chicken or vegetables; alternatively, toss it through pasta or rice or add to mashed potato for added colour and flavour.*

Spicy Bean Salsa

1/2 cup/125 g canned or cooked butter or navy beans

1/2 cup/180 g canned or cooked pinto or red kidney beans

1 cob sweet corn, kernels removed or 1/2 cup/100 g canned no-added-salt sweet corn kernels, drained

1/2 red onion, diced

1 plum tomato, diced

1 small jalapeño chilli, finely chopped

1 teaspoon ground coriander

1 cup/250 mL low-salt chicken stock

chopped fresh parsley or chives

Place butter beans, pinto beans, sweet corn, onion, tomato, chilli, coriander and chicken stock in a saucepan. Bring to the boil. Strain. Cool. Stir in parsley. Cover. Store in the refrigerator for up to 5 days.

Makes 2 cups/500 mL

68 kilojoules/16 Calories – per 1 tablespoon
less than 1 g total fat; nil saturated fat; 26 mg sodium

Cook's tip: *Use this salsa as an accompaniment to grilled polenta, chicken, veal or pork or as a dip for vegetables.*

Other Salsa Combinations

Many seasonal herbs, fruit or vegetables can be used in salsas. It all depends on what you are serving. Following are a few other ideas to get you thinking and creating.

Corn and Red Pepper Salsa: Roast a cob of sweet corn and a red pepper in a hot oven or on the barbecue for 10 minutes or until charred and soft. Using the back of a knife, remove kernels from the corn cob and place in a bowl. Peel the red pepper and dice. Place in bowl with corn. Add some chopped fresh basil, a splash of olive oil and balsamic vinegar and black pepper to taste. Toss to combine. Serve with pasta, fish, chicken or bread.

Fruity Tropical Mint Salsa: Place diced fresh peaches or pineapple, chopped red onion, a few chopped unsalted cashews, almonds or macadamias, chopped fresh mint, a splash of white wine vinegar and a little grated orange zest in a bowl. Toss. Serve with grilled lamb, pork or prawns, or toss through a rice salad.

Orange and Onion Salsa: Place diced orange, chopped red onion, chopped fresh mint, cider vinegar and freshly ground black pepper to taste in a bowl. Toss to combine. Serve with grilled meat, chicken or seafood.

Rockmelon and Green Pepper Salsa: Place diced rockmelon, chopped green pepper, chopped green onion, shredded fresh basil, lime juice and freshly ground black pepper to taste in a bowl. Toss to combine. Serve with salmon, trout or as part of an antipasto platter.

Berry and Ginger Salsa: Place blueberries or cranberries, minced fresh ginger, finely chopped mild green chilli or green pepper and honey in a bowl. Toss to combine. Delicious served with game.

Tomato Sauce

2 teaspoons olive oil

1 onion, finely chopped

1 garlic clove, crushed

125 g no-added-salt tomato paste

1 kg diced ripe tomatoes, preferably plum, peeled and diced
or 2 x 425 g canned no-added-salt diced tomatoes

3 tablespoons chopped fresh basil

1 tablespoon chopped fresh parsley

1 teaspoon brown sugar or honey

1 bay leaf

2 cups/500 mL hot low-salt chicken stock (page 174)

$1/2$ teaspoon freshly ground black pepper

1   Place oil, onion and garlic in a nonstick frying pan over a medium heat. Cook, stirring, for 3-4 minutes or until onion is soft and translucent.

2   Stir in tomato paste. Cook, for 3-4 minutes or until mixture becomes deep red and develops a rich aroma.

3   Stir in tomatoes, basil, parsley, sugar, bay leaf, stock and black pepper. Bring to simmering. Cook, stirring occasionally for $1^1/2$ hours. Remove bay leaf and discard. Cool slightly.

4   Place tomato mixture in a food processor. Purée. Alternatively, push mixture through a sieve. Check and adjust seasoning. Store in an airtight container in the refrigerator for up to 1 week.

Makes 4 cups/1 litre

31 kilojoules/7 Calories – per 1 tablespoon
less than 1 g total fat; nil saturated fat; 15 mg sodium

Barbecue sauce: To make a rich and flavoursome barbecue sauce, add chilli or tabasco sauce to taste and instead of the chicken stock, use 1 cup/250 mL strong black coffee, $1/2$ cup/ 125 mL cider, $1/4$ cup/60 mL cider vinegar and 2 tablespoons no-added-salt worcestershire sauce.

Author's note: *These sauces are a great alternative to the commercial varieties. The tomato sauce can be used in place of purée in pasta dishes, casseroles or soups. Both sauces are great served with barbecued or grilled meats. For a creamy tomato sauce, stir in a little evaporated skim milk.*

Cucumber Yogurt Sauce

$1/2$ cup/90 g grated cucumber

1 tablespoon chopped fresh dill or mint

1 cup/200 g low-fat natural yogurt

1 tablespoon lime or lemon juice

freshly ground black pepper

Place cucumber, dill, yogurt, lime juice and black pepper to taste in a bowl. Mix to combine. Cover. Refrigerate until ready to serve. Best used within a day of making.

Makes $1^1/2$ cups/375 mL

50 kilojoules/12 Calories – per 2 tablespoons
less than 1 g total fat; nil saturated fat; 15 mg sodium

Cook's tip: *Serve this sauce with seafood dishes, grilled vegetables or as a dip with hot bread.*

Mustard Vinaigrette

$^1/_4$ cup/60 mL low-salt stock (page 174), fruit juice or wine

2 tablespoons red wine vinegar

2 tablespoons extra virgin olive oil

2 teaspoons wholegrain or dijon mustard

freshly ground black pepper

Place stock, vinegar, oil, mustard and black pepper to taste in a screwtop jar. Shake well to combine. Store in the refrigerator for up to 7 days. Bring to room temperature before using.
Makes $^1/_2$ cup/125 mL

199 kilojoules/48 Calories – per 1 tablespoon
2 g total fat; less than 1 g saturated fat; 5 mg sodium

Cook's tip: *Use this as a basic recipe and add flavourings such as chopped fresh herbs, citrus peel, spices and diced vegetables to suit. This tangy dressing is great for salads or spooned over grilled meat, fish or vegetables.*

Creamy Sour Dressing

$^1/_2$ cup/125 g reduced-fat ricotta cheese

1 cup/200 g low-fat natural yogurt

2 tablespoons red wine vinegar

2 teaspoons lemon or lime juice

2 teaspoons no-added-salt tomato sauce, optional

Place ricotta cheese in a blender or food processor. Purée. Add yogurt, vinegar, lemon juice and tomato sauce. Process to combine. Cover. Store in the refrigerator for up to 4 days.
Makes 1$^1/_2$ cups/375 mL

128 kilojoules/31 Calories – per 2 tablespoons
1 g total fat; 1 g saturated fat; 53 mg sodium

Cook's tip: *Add to this basic recipe seasonings such as freshly ground black pepper, chopped fresh herbs or diced vegetables. Use this low-fat alternative as a creamy salad dressing for coleslaw or Caesar salad, spooned over baked jacket potatoes, as a dip for prawns or in place of mayonnaise or sour cream.*

Traditional Balsamic Dressing

2 teaspoons wholegrain mustard

$^1/_4$ cup/60 g balsamic vinegar

1 tablespoon olive oil

1 tablespoon orange or apple juice or low-salt stock of your choice

freshly ground black pepper

Place mustard, vinegar, oil, juice and black pepper to taste in a screwtop jar. Shake well to combine. Store in the refrigerator for up to 7 days. Bring to room temperature before using.
Makes $^1/_3$ cup/90 mL

200 kilojoules/48 Calories – per 1 tablespoon
5 g total fat; 1 g saturated fat; 1 mg sodium

Author's note: *All over Europe and now Australia, the USA and England, restaurant tables are decorated with bottles of oil and balsamic vinegar, so you can dress your own salads or use instead of butter on bread. Balsamic vinegar dressings are commonly added to salads and usually have a lot more oil than vinegar. For those who prefer to moderate their use of oil, I prepared this dressing that tastes just as good as its high-oil cousin. Using concentrated fruit juice or stock gives the dressing body and reduces its tartness.*

stocks

Making your own stock may seem time-consuming, especially with the range of liquid and powdered stocks now available. However, there's nothing quite like the flavour of homemade stock, you always know what's in it and there's a lot less salt! You can also concentrate it and store it in ice cube trays for a whole range of uses, from dressings to casseroles or just to have on hand to add flavour to stir-fries or rice dishes.

Storing stock: When preparing stock for storage, strain the hot stock through rinsed cheesecloth or muslin into a stainless steel bowl, then place bowl in iced water. Stir occasionally to speed the cooling process. If you plan to use the stock within a day or two, store in a covered container in the refrigerator. Alternatively, place in a freezerproof container, seal, label and date. Store in the freezer – remember to leave 2 cm at the top of the container for expansion during freezing.

Concentrated stock: If you wish to concentrate the stock, return strained stock to a clean saucepan and boil until stock is reduced to one-quarter of its original volume. Freeze in ice cube trays. Once frozen, turn out of ice cube trays and place in freezer bags. Use as required.

Chicken Stock

1 kg chicken or turkey bones

1 carrot, chopped

1 onion, chopped

1 stalk celery, including tops, chopped

1 sprig fresh parsley

1 sprig fresh thyme

1 teaspoon black peppercorns

1 bay leaf

1   Remove any excess fat from bones. Rinse under cold water. Place bones in a stock pot or large saucepan. Pour over water to cover – you will need 4-6 cups/1-1.5 litres.

2   Place pan over a high heat. Bring to the boil. Reduce heat. Simmer, skimming foam from top as necessary, for 1 hour. Add water as required to maintain a constant volume.

3   Add carrot, onion, celery, parsley, thyme, peppercorns and bay leaf. Simmer for 3-4 hours. Skim foam from top as necessary and add water as required to maintain a constant volume.

4   Strain. Cool as quickly as possible. Cover. Chill overnight. Lift fat from surface. Discard. Refrigerate or freeze.

200 kilojoules/48 Calories – analysis for whole quantity
less than 1 g total fat; nil saturated fat; 60 mg sodium

Fish Stock

1 teaspoon light olive oil

few drops sesame oil, optional

500 g fish bones and/or prawn shells

1 leek, chopped

1 stalk celery, chopped

1/2 cup/45 g chopped mushrooms

1 teaspoon black peppercorns

1 sprig fresh thyme or oregano

1 sprig fresh parsley

150 mL dry white wine

1   Heat olive and sesame oils together in a stockpot or large saucepan over a low heat. Add fish bones, leek and celery. Cook, stirring occasionally, until leek is soft and mixture becomes aromatic, but not brown.

2   Add mushrooms, black peppercorns, thyme, parsley and wine. Pour over enough cold water to cover – you will need 2 1/2-3 cups/600-750 mL. Bring to the boil. Reduce heat. Simmer for 20-25 minutes. Skim foam from top as necessary.

3   Strain. Complete as described in step 4 of Chicken Stock.

746 kilojoules/186 Calories – analysis for whole quantity
5 g total fat; less than 1 g saturated fat; 70 mg sodium

Brown Beef or Veal Stock

1 kg beef or veal bones

2 teaspoons olive oil

1 onion, chopped

1 carrot, chopped

1 small leek, chopped

1 stalk celery, chopped

¼ cup/60 mL no-added-salt tomato paste

1 bay leaf

1 sprig fresh thyme

1 teaspoon black peppercorns

1   Preheat oven to 190°C. Remove any fat from bones. Place bones in a roasting dish. Roast for 20 minutes until bones are brown.

2   Heat oil in a stock pot or large saucepan over a medium heat. Add onion, carrot, leek and celery. Cook, stirring, for 4-5 minutes or until vegetables are soft.

3   Stir in tomato paste. Cook for 3-4 minutes or until mixture becomes deep red and develops a rich aroma.

4   Add bones, bay leaf, thyme and black peppercorns to pan. Pour over water to cover – you will need 5-6 cups/1.25-1.5 litres. Bring to boil. Reduce heat. Simmer for 6-7 hours. Skim foam from top as necessary and add water as required to maintain a constant volume.

5   Strain. Complete as described in step 4 of Chicken Stock.

878 kilojoules/211 Calories – analysis for whole quantity
11 g total fat; 1 g saturated fat; 145 mg sodium

Vegetable Stock

1 teaspoon unsaturated oil

1 clove garlic, crushed

1 shallot, chopped

1 carrot, chopped

½ cup/45 g sliced mushrooms

1 stalk celery, including top, chopped

½ cup/70 g sliced fennel

⅓ cup/50 g sliced leeks

1 sprig fresh parsley

1 sprig fresh thyme

1 bay leaf

½ teaspoon crushed black peppercorns

4 cups/1 litre water

100 mL dry vermouth

1   Place oil, garlic and shallot in a stockpot or large saucepan over a low heat. Cook, stirring, until garlic is soft, but not brown.

2   Add carrot, mushrooms, celery, fennel, leeks, parsley, thyme, bay leaf, peppercorns, water and vermouth. Bring to the boil. Reduce heat. Simmer for 45 minutes. Skim foam from top as necessary and add water as required to maintain a constant volume.

3   Strain. Complete as described in step 4 of Chicken Stock.

817 kilojoules/196 Calories – analysis for whole quantity
5 g total fat; less than 1 g saturated fat; 86 mg sodium

miscellaneous basics

Homemade Corn Chips

large corn or wheat tortillas

unsaturated oil

seasonings of your choice, such as ground paprika or coriander, black pepper, chopped fresh oregano or sesame seeds, optional

1   Preheat oven to 200°C. Lightly brush or spray tortillas with oil. Sprinkle with seasoning of your choice.

2   Cut each tortilla into eight wedges. Place in a single layer on baking trays. Bake for 8-10 minutes or until wedges are crisp and golden. Transfer to wire racks to cool. Store in an airtight container for up to 1 week.

70 kilojoules/17 Calories – per wedge
less than 1 g total fat; nil saturated fat; 32 mg sodium

Author's note: *Use these as a low-fat alternative to commercial corn chips. In this book I have served with the White Bean Nachos (page 38), or serve with dips or crumbled over soups and casseroles for added crunch.*

Yogurt Cheese

3 cups/600 g low-fat natural yogurt

seasonings of your choice, such as chopped fresh herbs, ground spices, chopped fresh chilli or grated vegetables

1   Line a colander with a double thickness of cheesecloth or muslin. Place over a large bowl. Spoon in yogurt. Cover with plastic food wrap. Stand in the refrigerator overnight.

2   Transfer yogurt to a clean bowl. Discard whey. Add seasonings of your choice to cheese. Mix to combine. Store cheese in an airtight container in the refrigerator for up to 1 week.
Makes 1 cup/250 mL

67 kilojoules/16 Calories – per 1 tablespoon
less than 1 g total fat; nil saturated fat; 21 mg sodium

Suggested uses: *Yogurt cheese is a great base for dips and sauces and for serving with vegetables. Can also be used as a substitute for sour cream in these types of recipes. Interesting vegetable flavourings include grated cucumber, raw beetroot or cooked mashed pumpkin. For a sweet variation, add diced fresh fruit and honey or sugar and use as an accompaniment with desserts or as a spread on scones.*

Tabbouleh

1 cup/170 g burghul (cracked wheat)

1/2 cup/60 g finely chopped white or green onion

3 tomatoes, diced

1 cup/30 g chopped fresh parsley

1/2 cup/10 g chopped fresh mint

LEMON DRESSING

1/3 cup/90 mL lemon juice

2 teaspoons olive oil

freshly ground black pepper

1   Place burghul in a bowl. Pour over boiling water to cover. Stand for 45-60 minutes or until the grains swell and soften.

2   Drain. Press to remove excess moisture. Place in a salad bowl. Add tomatoes, parsley and mint to burghul. Toss.

3   **Dressing:** Place lemon juice, oil and black pepper to taste in a screwtop jar. Shake well to combine. Pour salad. Toss. Cover. Refrigerate until ready to use. Keeps for 2-3 days.
Serves 6

465 kilojoules/112 Calories – per serve
2 g total fat; less than 1 g saturated fat; 6 mg sodium

Hummus

2 1/2 cups/400 g cooked or canned chickpeas, rinsed and drained

4 tablespoons tahini (sesame seed paste)

3 cloves garlic, chopped

juice of 2-3 lemons

2 tablespoons olive oil

freshly ground black pepper

1   Place chickpeas, tahini, garlic, lemon juice, oil and black pepper to taste in a food processor or blender. Purée. Add a little water or vegetable or chicken stock if you like a thinner consistency. Check seasoning. Add more garlic, lemon juice or black pepper if necessary.

2   To serve as a dip, place hummus in a bowl. Sprinkle with paprika or chopped fresh parsley. Accompany with a selection of raw vegetables and Lebanese or Turkish bread. Alternatively, use as a spread instead of butter.
Makes 1 1/2 cups/375 mL

594 kilojoules/43 Calories – per 2 tablespoons
11 g total fat; 1 g saturated fat; 11 mg sodium

Lemon Yogurt Icing

1 cup/155 g icing sugar, sifted

1 tablespoon low-fat natural yogurt

1/2 teaspoon finely grated lemon zest

1/2 teaspoon fresh lemon juice

water

Place icing sugar, yogurt, lemon zest and juice in a bowl or food processor. Mix or process until smooth. If necessary, slowly add water until you have an icing of spreading consistency.

1281 kilojoules/315 Calories – analysis for total quantity
nil total fat; nil saturated fat; 14 mg sodium

Cook's tip: *The icing may be stored in an airtight container in the refrigerator for 4-5 days – before using, add warm water until it is of spreadable consistency.*

magic**menus**

Summer Sunday Brunch for 4

Rockmelon and Rocket Salad (page 100)

Tuscan Bread Salad with Poached Trout (page 104)

Rosemary, Lemon and Pine Nut Bread (page 160)

Frozen Mango Blush (page 148)

Make-Ahead Outdoor Lunch for 6

Italian Meatloaf (page 126) – serve cold

Orange and Almond Couscous Salad (page 72)

Tuscan Vegetable Terrine (page 36)

A large bowl of mixed salad greens

Italian or sourdough bread

Platter of fresh fruit and reduced-fat fresh ricotta cheese

An Intimate Picnic for 2

Niçoise Tuna Baguettes (page 34)

Oakleaf, Pear and Walnut Salad (page 46)

Pistachio and Almond Amaretti (page 156)

A bottle of sparkling mineral water

A bottle of crisp fruity white wine

A Mid-winter Dinner Party for 4

Creamy Oyster Bisque (page 18) or Mussels with
Tomatoes and Wine (page 132)

Pork Medallions with Winter Fruits (page 124)

A bowl of steamed baby squash and asparagus

Orange and Blueberry Upside Down Cakes (page 144)

An Easter Family Meal for 6

Lemon and Broccoli Risotto (page 96)

Salmon Vegetable Parcels (page 62)

Poached Ricotta Pears (page 140)

A salad of mixed greens tossed with Mustard
Vinaigrette (page 173)

Italian bread

Turkish Fig Sweets (page 144)

A Christmas Seafood for 8

Asparagus Parmesan Pastry Spirals (page 108)

Roast Beet and Smoked Trout Salad (page 34)

Barbecued Seafood Salad (page 70)

Swordfish and Pineapple Kebabs (page 70)

Orange and Almond Couscous Salad (page 72)

Layer Fruit Mould (page 140) served with Custard Cream
(page 142 with recipe for Hazelnut Filo Baskets) – made
using brandy instead of vanilla essence

Bon Bons

A bottle of champagne

Sunday Night Meal for 2

Yellow Pepper Soup with Red Pepper Harissa (page 18)

Baked Chicken and Vegetable Lavash Rolls (page 42)

Dried Fruit Sandwiches (page 158)

Coffee

Summer Cocktail Party Ideas

Blinis with Herbed Yogurt Cheese (page 22)

Gravlax Spirals (page 30)

White Bean Nachos with Roast Tomato Salsa (page 38)

Sushi Hand Rolls (page 46)

Tuna Carpaccio in Witlof Leaves (page 102)

Winter Cocktail Party Ideas

Baked Ricotta Mushrooms (page 30)

Asparagus Parmesan Pastry Spirals (page 108)

Moroccan Lemon Chicken Shish Kebabs (page 24)

Oyster Spring Rolls (page 26)

An Impromptu Dinner Party for 4

A bowl of dry roasted nuts and rice crackers

Lemon Myrtle Scented Fish cooked in Paper (page 56)

Steamed jasmine rice

Stir-fried Fruit (page 138) served with purchased lemon gelato

Vegetarian Banquet

Caribbean Gazpacho with Avocado Cream (page 16)

Mixed Mushroom and Goat's Cheese Strudel (page 40)

Baked Ratatouille and Penne (page 132)

Rice, Vegetable and Feta Strata (page 36)

Stir-fried Fruit served with Lychee and Lemon Grass Ice Cream (page 138)

Pizza Party for 6

Red Onion, Red Pepper and Rocket Pizza (page 102)

Fresh Salmon and Dill Pizza (page 102)

Rockmelon and Rocket Salad (page 100)

A salad of mixed greens tossed with Traditional Balsamic Dressing (page 173)

Coffee and Ginger Almond Bread (page 158)

A Ladies Afternoon Tea Party

Blinis with Herbed Yogurt Cheese (page 22) – topped with smoked salmon

Cherry and Walnut Teacake (page 162)

Macadamia and Coffee Marzipan (page 142)

Coffee and Ginger Almond Bread (page 158)

Currant and Buttermilk Scones with Orange Blossom Cream (page 164)

A Backyard Barbecue for 6

Grilled Asparagus and Mushroom Bruschetta (page 68)

Warm Barbecued Octopus and Potato Salad (page 66)

Mediterranean Pork and Apple Burgers (page 76)

Frozen Mango Blush (page 148)

Ideas for Sports Enthusiasts

The following high-carbohydrate recipes are great choices for sportspeople. Remember to serve with lots of steamed vegetables or salad with a low-fat dressing and additional bread or rolls, if necessary.

Salmon and Potato Lasagne (page 38)

Fettuccine Caprese (page 98)

Calamari and Coriander Spaghetti (page 50)

Lemon and Broccoli Risotto (page 96)

Sweet Potato and Cannellini Falafel (page 68)

Apricot Risotto (page 146)

blood cholesterol levels

If you have too much cholesterol in your blood, it can settle on the inside wall of your blood vessels. As it builds up, the blood vessels become clogged and eventually blocked. This process is known as atherosclerosis and may result in a heart attack or stroke.

There are two main types of blood cholesterol (also known as lipids) – HDL (high density lipoprotein) and LDL (low density lipoprotein).

HDL CHOLESTEROL

This is known as the 'good' cholesterol. It tends to protect against heart disease by clearing cholesterol from the arteries. If a higher proportion of your total cholesterol is HDL cholesterol, then you are at less risk of heart disease. Regular exercisers, non-smokers and pre-menopausal women tend to have higher HDL levels.

LDL CHOLESTEROL

This is known as the 'bad' cholesterol. It tends to build up and clog the arteries.

TRIGLYCERIDES

There is another type of fat in blood known as triglycerides. High-blood triglyceride levels are also known to contribute to heart disease. Regular exercise, maintaining a healthy body weight, and eating a diet low in saturated fat will help keep your triglyceride levels down. Drinking too much alcohol can lead to high triglyceride levels.

There are many factors to consider when deciding what your levels of total cholesterol, HDL and LDL cholesterol should be. These include your age, family history and whether or not you have other heart disease risk factors such as diabetes or hypertension.

Eating a healthy diet low in fat, especially saturated fats, will help keep your blood lipid levels in the healthy range. Some people may require lipid-lowering medications in addition to lifestyle modifications. The following table can be used as a guide, but you should talk to your doctor to clarify this.

GUIDE TO BLOOD FAT LEVELS				
RISK CATEGORIES	TARGET LIPID LEVELS (MMOL/LITRE) FASTING			
	total cholesterol	HDL	LDL	Triglycerides
I Existing heart disease	<4.5	>1.0	<2.5	<2.0
II Diabetes, hypertension, smoking or family history of heart disease or high blood cholesterol	<5.0	>1.0	<3.0	<2.0
III All others	<6.0	>1.0	<4.0	<4.0

Adapted from the Heart Foundation's 'Guide for the Use of Lipid-Lowering Drugs in Adults' 1998

cholesterol in foods

To lower your blood cholesterol level, it is much more important to look at your saturated fat intake than the amount of cholesterol you eat. Saturated fats affect your blood cholesterol levels more than cholesterol in food. Furthermore, cholesterol in food (dietary cholesterol) mostly occurs in combination with other saturated fats in food. Therefore, reducing your overall saturated fat intake will almost certainly reduce your cholesterol intake.

There are just a few foods which are not high in fat but which still contain considerable amounts of cholesterol. These include eggs and offal meats. An area of contention is whether or not it is necessary to limit

some seafoods. Prawns, scampi, calamari (squid) and octopus are a little higher in cholesterol than other seafoods. However, they are also a good source of Omega-3 fats, therefore many experts now believe these seafoods should not be restricted.

If you are trying to lower your blood cholesterol level it is therefore recommended that you:

- *limit eggs to no more than 2-3 a week; and*
- *limit brains, liver, kidney, paté, sweetbread and tongue.*

If your blood cholesterol level is normal you do not need to limit these foods.

flavour with less fat

Embarking on a healthy style of eating will unfold a whole new world of flavours and you'll soon find that your tastes and preferences will change. The first few weeks and even months, however, can be challenging as you attempt to find ways of reducing and improving the type of fat you use, while enjoying your meals Many people give up at this stage, but take heart, there are a few secrets to creating meals that look and taste as good as they are for you. These tips for substituting some commonly used higher fat foods with more desirable ingredients will give your meals the textures and flavours you are used to, yet be better for you. (See Simply Healthy Eating page 0 for more information on fats.)

meat and chicken

Some people complain that meat trimmed of fat or chicken without skin is hard to cook, becomes tough and lacks flavour, however with a little care, it's easy to have moist and flavoursome lean meat.

CASSEROLES, SOUPS AND STEWS
Use lean cuts of meat. Trim of visible fat before cooking. Marinating and searing meat helps to keep leaner cuts tender and moist. Bulk up casseroles, soups and stews with beans and grains. If you have time, chill before serving, so that you can lift any fat off the top.

ROASTS
Trim of visible fat before cooking. Cook meat on a rack set in a roasting dish so the fat drains away. Keep the meat moist and flavoursome by brushing with a marinade during cooking. Don't overcook as this toughens leaner cuts of meat.

GRILLING OR BARBECUEING
Trim of visible fat before cooking. Marinate and brush with marinade during cooking. Sear on a high heat and don't overcook.

dressings

Dressings are taking up an increasing amount of room on supermarket shelves and many of these are low in fat. Making your own is easy, you can adapt them to suit your tastes and they will contain a lot less salt. Try using ingredients such as juices, yogurt, buttermilk, mustards, vinegars, stocks, puréed vegetables and flavoursome oils. There are many examples of low-fat dressings and sauces throughout this book. Many can be used to accompany other foods.

pastry

This doesn't have to be taken off your menu and there are three recipes in The Basics chapter (page 168) for low-fat sweet and savoury pastries. Try using filo pastry for making parcels and rolls or cases for fruit desserts. Brush every few sheets with a little oil or low-fat natural yogurt if you like, but it can also be used plain. Try lavash bread for wrapping around savoury fillings before baking – for some ideas see page 42. Cooked seasoned rice pressed into a pie dish makes a great alternative to pastry for pies and quiches. Damper or scone dough also works well for savoury pies or fruit scrolls and is lower in fat than puff or Danish pastry.

high-fat dairy foods

Dairy foods play an important role in a healthy diet. They are rich in calcium and contain protein and many vitamins and minerals. It's just a matter of choosing the lower fat ones.

BUTTER
This is easy to reduce. On sandwiches, try ricotta or cottage cheese, mustard, jam, relish, chutney, mashed avocado and yogurt. Brush toast with virgin olive oil – it's still high in fat, but a better fat and you need only a little. There are many cakes which can be made using oil or nut and fruit based mixes. Scones and teacakes made with buttermilk as the liquid and no fat at all are light and fluffy. For some ideas see the selection of recipes in this book starting on page 152.

Instead of using a butter and flour base for thickening sauces and casseroles, dissolve cornflour or arrowroot in a little liquid and stir in just before serving.

LIQUID CREAM
In sauces and desserts, replace cream with evaporated skim milk. Ricotta cheese blended with icing sugar, vanilla or fruit makes a great substitute for whipped cream, see recipe for Orange Blossom Cream (page 164). Instead of rich double cream, try low-fat frûche or the extra rich yogurt – it's higher in fat than most yogurts with 6-7% fat, but still a lot lower than double cream.

SOUR CREAM
You'll be hard pressed to notice the difference when you use low-fat natural yogurt instead of sour cream. It works in most recipes from dips to sauces and casseroles or on baked potato, but add it during the last stage of cooking or blend with a little cornflour, as it separates if allowed to boil. For a rich, creamy texture use Yogurt Cheese (page 176)

CHEESES
There are a huge variety of reduced-fat options, but you need to read the label as the claims can be deceptive. For sandwiches, fruit plates and on pizza, try bocconcini or reduced-fat mozzarella and crumble reduced-fat and -salt feta or goat's cheese or baked ricotta cheese in salads and pasta sauces. Choose an intensely flavoured cheese such as parmesan when just a few shavings are needed on top of risotto, pasta or a casserole. Combine grated cheese with rolled oats, wheatgerm or other grains to make it go further without extra fat.

MILK AND BUTTER BASED WHITE SAUCES
Traditionally used for dishes such as vegetables and pasta, white sauces can be made with skim or evaporated skim milk and thickened with cornflour. Or try puréeing white butter beans with low-fat milk and a little wine or stock for a thick and creamy alternative. For a creamy pasta sauce, toss fresh ricotta cheese through hot pasta.

ICE CREAM
This is perhaps the easiest change, thanks to the many innovative manufacturers who have created a range of low-fat options. Look for ice creams with less than 5% fat or sorbets and experiment with your own flavourings see the recipe for Lemon Grass and Lychee Ice Cream on page 138.

deep frying

Deep frying is a messy and time-consuming method of cooking. There are many alternative ways for making crisp chips, crumbed fish or crusty chicken. For crispy potatoes and root vegetables, lightly brush or spray pre-steamed vegetables with unsaturated oil. Bake at 220°C oven until crisp. Coat fish and chicken with corn or oat flake crumbs and bake. Polenta, couscous and ground nuts combined with herbs are other choices for crispy coatings.

coconut milk

High in saturated fat, coconut milk is a common ingredient in Thai and Indian cooking. As an alternative, use evaporated skim milk flavoured with a few drops of coconut essence or boil some desiccated coconut in water or skim milk for 30 minutes, strain and use.

the simply healthy kitchen

the tools

A GOOD SET OF SHARP KNIVES
Makes cooking easier and faster. Trimming fat from meat and slicing vegetables becomes a breeze! Preserve their life and quality: store in a wooden knife block; use only on a board; and sharpen regularly.

GOOD QUALITY BRISTLE PASTRY BRUSHES
Have many uses including: brushing flavourings such as vinegar and mustard over food before grilling or roasting; brushing bread and scones with egg white and/or milk before cooking; and brushing oil onto the surface of frying pans, cake tins and food before cooking.

NONSTICK BAKING PAPER
Can be used to give baking dishes a nonstick surface or instead of fat in cake tins and on baking trays. Food wrapped in baking paper and cooked in the oven steams in its own juices – it is a healthy and delicious way to cook fish and chicken.

NONSTICK SAUCEPANS AND FRYING PANS
Are invaluable for low-fat cooking, as little or no fat is required. Invest in good quality pans in a range of sizes to suit your cooking needs. And only use wooden or plastic utensils to maintain the surface.

A WOK
Essential for Asian cooking and stir-frying. Nonstick woks are available and a good investment for the healthy cook.

A RIDGED CAST IRON GRILL PAN
Also called a char-grilled pan, this pan requires little or no added fat, and as the food sits on the ridges, any fat drains away during cooking. They can be heated to a very high heat, which gives food a delicious, slightly charred flavour and helps seal in the juices.

A SLOTTED SPOON
Use for lifting cooked foods from the cooking water, so you can re-use the water. Also ideal for lifting the fat off the surface of soups, casseroles and stocks.

A FOOD PROCESSOR
Use a large one for puréeing soups and desserts, making your own lean mince, quick mix low-fat cakes, pastries and breads and pasta sauces. For grinding nuts, chopping small quantities of herbs and whipping up pesto, salsas and dressings, a small one is better. Units which incorporate a number of features, such as a processor, blender, juicer, beaters and an attachment for processing smaller quantities, take up less room in the kitchen and give you lots of appliances in one.

basic ingredients

Use this list as a guide and add your own must-haves. Remember where possible to choose the low- or reduced-fat and/or salt varieties.

RICE
Keep a variety for different uses. Calrose for Asian dishes and desserts; jasmine to accompany Thai meals; basmati to serve with Indian food; arborio for risottos; long grain for salads; wild rice to give a nutty taste and an added visual effect. Cooked rice keeps in the refrigerator for several days. It also freezes well and can be reheated in the microwave.

PASTA
Keep a variety of pasta shapes for different uses. A good basic selection would include: one or two ribbon pastas such as fettuccine and spaghetti; a short pasta such as macaroni or penne; and lasagne sheets. Leftover pasta freezes well and can be reheated in the microwave.

BEANS AND LENTILS
Canned, vacuum-packed and dried legumes all have the same nutritional value, however, canned varieties may contain added salt. If using canned legumes, rinse and drain before using to remove excess salt. They are low in fat, a good source of fibre and a main protein source for non-meat meals. Also use for adding bulk to casseroles and soups.

A SELECTION OF CEREALS AND GRAINS
Rolled oats, wheat germ, buckwheat, barley, cracked wheat and other grains and cereals are a low-fat way to

add bulk and fibre to dishes such as casseroles and soups. With the increased interest in ethnic cuisines, cereals such as couscous and quinoa have become popular. They are naturally low-fat, quick to prepare and make a great alternative to rice, pasta or potatoes.

MONO- AND POLYUNSATURATED OILS
Use olive, canola and unsaturated oils for general cooking and brushing of cake tins and grills. To add flavour to dressings and grilled foods, add or brush with a little extra virgin olive, macadamia, sesame or other flavoured oil – remember you only need a touch.

CANNED AND/OR FROZEN VEGETABLES
When choosing canned vegetables go for the no-added-salt varieties. If unable to find these, rinse and drain vegetables such as corn kernels and peas before using. Rinsing removes some, but not all, of the salt. Canned tomatoes are the basis of many casseroles, soups and quick sauces. Canned or frozen vegetables can add nutritional value and colour to dishes.

TOMATO PASTE
Remember to choose the no-added-salt variety. Use to add flavour to sauces, soups and casseroles and for spreading on pizzas and flatbreads.

FAVOURITE HERBS AND SPICES
Keep a selection of dried, bottled and fresh herbs and spices to hand. Bottled chopped lemon grass, chillies ginger and garlic are convenient and easy to use.

WHOLE PEPPERCORNS
An essential flavouring for adding flavour and spice without fat. You might like to have one grinder for black peppercorns and one for white peppercorns. White pepper is good for pale colour foods.

A SELECTION OF CONDIMENTS
Use mustards, horseradish, pickles and chutneys as: spreads instead of butter; for adding flavour to grilled meat and fish; and to give sauces, dressings and casseroles a flavour boost. As many are high in salt, use sparingly and if possible, select reduced- or low-salt varieties. Also check labels for hidden fats and salts.

A VARIETY OF VINEGARS
Use to add flavour to low-fat dressings, sauces, soups and casseroles. Include balsamic, red wine, rice, cider and herbed vinegars in your pantry.

A VARIETY OF SAUCES
Choose sauces to suit your cooking style. Where possible, select reduced- or low-fat and -salt varieties. Remember to read the labels for hidden fats and salts.

CANNED AND/OR FROZEN FRUIT
Use for quick desserts or snacks. For a low-fat dessert sauce, simply purée and add spices of your choice.

DRIED FRUIT
Use to add sweetness, texture and nutritional value to sweet and savoury dishes (e.g. meatloaves, casseroles, rice and pasta dishes). Also a great low-fat snack.

A SELECTION OF NUTS
Use to add texture and flavour to a variety of dishes, or just as a healthy snack. With the exception of coconut, nuts contain mostly unsaturated fats. However, because of their high oil content, you shouldn't overindulge if you are concerned about your weight, but they are a better option than a slab of cheese or chocolate.

COCOA POWDER
Low in fat, it has a characteristic bitterness that adds richness and colour to sauces, cakes and biscuits, or combine with skim milk to make a low-fat smoothie.

WINE, SHERRY AND PORT
Adds flavour to many dishes. If you're concerned about the alcohol, remember it evaporates during cooking. Use wine and sherry in marinades, and port is delicious for macerating dried fruit.

EVAPORATED SKIM MILK
A must-have for those who like creamy sauces and soups. Use it instead of sour cream or cream in sauces, soups, casseroles and dressings. When chilled, it can be whipped like cream, however, it does not hold for as long and is best used straight away.

LOW-FAT NATURAL YOGURT AND/OR BUTTERMILK
Use for quick dressings and sauces instead of sour cream or mayonnaise. Low-fat scones and cakes will be lighter if made with buttermilk instead of milk.

LOW-FAT RICOTTA AND/OR COTTAGE CHEESE
Use as a spread or whipped with puréed fruit to make an easy dessert. Makes a great low-fat substitute for cream and cream cheese in sauces and some baked products.

LOW-FAT ICE CREAM, GELATO OR SORBET
A great quick and healthy indulgence that even the kids will love.

PARMESAN CHEESE
Even though it's high in fat, Parmesan cheese is so flavoursome you only need a very small amount to add a flavour boost to pasta, rice and salads or casseroles. Buy in a piece and grate or shave as required. Remember to use sparingly.

glossary

AL DENTE
An Italian term meaning literally, to the tooth, and indicating the stage when pasta is cooked. It should be tender but with a slightly firm centre to the bite.

ARBORIO RICE
An Italian variety of rice with a high starch content that is ideal for risotto because it will develop a creamy texture without going mushy.

BOCCONCINI CHEESE
These small balls of fresh mozzarella cheese have a delightful delicate flavour with a creamy texture. Use in cooked dishes or salads. When cooked, it takes on the stringy characteristic of mozzarella. Having a high moisture content means it is lower in fat, however, it does not keep well and is best purchased as required. Available from delicatessens and some supermarkets.

BUCKWHEAT FLOUR
Often thought of as a grain, because of the way in which it is used, buckwheat is in fact a seed. Buckwheat flour is the ground seed and is available in light and dark varieties. Traditionally used to make blini and soba noodles.

BUTTERMILK
A slightly acidic, or yogurt-tasting liquid traditionally made from milk once the butter is removed and culture added. Low in fat and ideal for adding to smoothies, cakes, scones and dressings.

COUSCOUS
Tiny beads of ground semolina (a wheat product), low in fat. Most commonly available pre-cooked so you just need to add boiling water and soak for 10 minutes before steaming or using as desired.

DAIKON RADISH
A large, white, sweet tasting radish used frequently in Japanese cooking, but also delicious grated in salads and chopped for stir-fries.

GALANGAL
A member of the ginger family, galangal is used in South-East Asian (especially Thai) cooking. It can be purchased fresh from Asian food stores and some greengrocers and supermarkets. It is also available dried or in a bottled form.

GRAVLAX
Salmon which has been marinated in sugar, salt and sometimes dill. Sweeter and less salty than smoked salmon, gravlax is also made using ocean trout.

GREEN ONIONS
In this book, green onions refer to an immature onion with an unformed bulb and long green top. Depending on where you live, these onions may also be known as spring onions, shallots or scallions.

HUMMUS
A Middle Eastern paste made from chickpeas, tahini, olive oil, garlic and lemon juice.

KAFFIR LIME LEAVES
Most commonly available dried. These aromatic intensely fragrant leaves are used extensively in South-East Asian cooking.

MESCLUN
A mixture of green leaves.

MIRIN
Sweet rice wine used in Japanese cooking such as adding to rice, dipping sauces and marinades.

NORI (SUSHI-NORI)
Dried sheets of roasted seaweed used for wrapping sushi.

POLENTA
Fine grains made from ground corn (maize), used for making cornbread or cooked and served as you would rice. When cooled, it sets and can be sliced into wedges and grilled or baked.

QUINOA
Pronounced 'keen-wa'. This tiny South American grain has an interesting crunchy texture and delicate flavour. it is delicious in salads, or use as an alternative to rice. Always rinse before using to remove the bitter flavour. Quinoa can be purchased from most health food stores and some delicatessens and supermarkets.

SHALLOTS
The shallots used in this book are the French éschalot. These are small onions with a more delicate flavour than large onions. A similar type of shallot is also used in Asian cooking. Pickling onions can be used instead.

TOFU (BEAN CURD)
Pronounced dow-foo. This is a low fat, high protein, mild flavoured food made from boiled, crushed soybeans. It is purchased as a slab and can be soft or firm, depending on your use – stir-fry, grill, steam, add to soups, purée as a base for dips or use to make dairy-free cheesecakes. Being mild, it will take on whatever flavours you add.

index